Disjointed War

Military Operations in Kosovo, 1999

Bruce R. Nardulli, Walter L. Perry, Bruce Pirnie
John Gordon IV, John G. McGinn

T0312715

Prepared for the

United States Army

Approved for public release;
distribution unlimited

RAND

Arroyo Center

The research described in this report was sponsored by the United States Army under contract number DASW01-01-C-0003.

Library of Congress Cataloging-in-Publication Data

Disjointed war : military operations in Kosovo, 1999 / Bruce R. Nardulli ... [et al.].
  p. cm.
  "MR-1406."
  Includes bibliographical references.
  ISBN 0-8330-3096-5
  1. Kosovo (Serbia)—History—Civil War, 1998—Campaigns. 2. North Atlantic Treaty Organization—Armed Forces—Yugoslavia. I. Nardulli, Bruce R.

DR2087.5 .D57 2002
949.703—dc21

2002024817

Cover photos courtesy of U.S. Air Force Link (B2) at www.af.mil, and NATO Media Library (Round table Meeting) at www.nato.int.

RAND is a nonprofit institution that helps improve policy and decisionmaking through research and analysis. RAND® is a registered trademark. RAND's publications do not necessarily reflect the opinions or policies of its research sponsors.

Cover design by Stephen Bloodsworth

Published 2002 by RAND
1700 Main Street, P.O. Box 2138, Santa Monica, CA 90407-2138
1200 South Hayes Street, Arlington, VA 22202-5050
201 North Craig Street, Suite 102, Pittsburgh, PA 15213
RAND URL: http://www.rand.org/
To order RAND documents or to obtain additional information, contact Distribution Services: Telephone: (310) 451-7002;
Fax: (310) 451-6915; Email: order@rand.org

PREFACE

Following the 1999 Kosovo conflict, the Army asked RAND Arroyo Center to prepare an authoritative and detailed account of military operations with a focus on ground operations, especially Task Force Hawk. In response, the Arroyo Center delivered a classified report for use by the Army Staff and others with an interest in the Kosovo conflict. This document is an unclassified version of that report. The purpose is to offer the Army a more accessible document, while also reaching a wider audience. It should interest those concerned with employment of Army and joint forces. It should also interest those concerned with broader national security issues, especially the planning and conduct of contingency operations.

This research was sponsored jointly by the Director of Strategy, Plans, and Policy, Office of the Deputy Chief of Staff for Operations and Plans (G-3); the Director of the Center for Land Warfare (with sponsorship now assumed by the Director, Army Quadrennial Defense Review Office); Office of the Deputy Chief of Staff for Programs; and the Technical Advisor to the Deputy Chief of Staff for Operations and Plans. It was conducted in the Arroyo Center's Strategy, Doctrine, and Resources Program. The Arroyo Center is a federally funded research and development center sponsored by the United States Army.

For more information on RAND Arroyo Center, contact the Director of Operations (telephone 310-393-0411, extension 6500; FAX 310-451-6952; e-mail donnab@rand.org), or visit the Arroyo Center's Web site at http://www.rand.org/organization/ard/.

CONTENTS

FIGURES

TABLES

All military operations have problems, and NATO's Operation Allied Force was no exception. Nor did it accomplish every objective. But whatever problems plagued the operation, the outcome was a clear victory for NATO. Operation Allied Force compelled the Yugoslavs to end the ethnic cleansing and expulsion of Kosovar Albanians, withdraw their forces from Kosovo, accept an international military presence in the province, and permit the unconditional return of refugees. Arguably, it also compromised Slobodan Milosevic's ability to hold on to power and ultimately resulted in his incarceration.

All of that said, problems abounded during the NATO military operation, and this report focuses on these problems because they offer a rich trove of lessons for future operations. Specifically, we focus on a subset of problems, those implicit in our title "Disjointed War." Allied Force was a joint (multiservice) operation, but it was not fought that way—at least to the extent that it could and should have been. This was especially true when it came to joint planning and operations in integrating air and ground capabilities. Operation Allied Force was also a combined, multinational operation. Fighting as an alliance brought essential political benefits, but it also induced a host of issues that had important operational military implications. These joint and combined difficulties caused confusion, probably made the operation less effective than it could have been, and possibly delayed victory. Had Milosevic not capitulated and had the allies eventually decided to launch a ground offensive, this "disjointedness" could have had severe consequences.

A primary influence shaping the operation was the fact that at the outset none of the NATO countries had overriding national interests in the Kosovo crisis. True, conflict in the Balkans could spin out of control and create important problems for European nations, but national survival was not at stake. This absence of a vital interest shaped the allied response in fundamental ways. It fostered a cautious and incremental approach intended to minimize casualties and avoid any event that might make it difficult to walk away from the conflict if necessary. Substantial friendly casualties might have made it very difficult to withdraw, and this desire underpinned the decision to use only aircraft within restrictive operational guidelines.

THE JOINT APPROACH

Joint operations derive much of their effectiveness from the fact that they foreclose an opponent's options. Dispersing forces to keep them from becoming a lucrative target for air strikes typically leaves an opponent more vulnerable to piecemeal defeat on the ground. Concentrating combat units to increase their effectiveness in ground operations can increase their vulnerability to air attack. NATO's early decision for an air-only operation, which mirrored U.S. statements and sentiment, essentially ceded the initiative to Milosevic, enabling him to undertake his program of ethnic cleansing. His tactics of dispersion, coupled with concealment and sporadic use of his air defenses, effectively trumped the only card NATO was willing to play.

None of this is to minimize the host of problems that would have clustered around any decision to send ground forces into Kosovo or the advantages that the air-only approach offered. Indeed, the decision represented a pragmatic recognition that NATO had not mustered the political will to commit its ground forces and that, if anything were to be done, it had to be an air operation. Nonetheless, a sober explanation of the limitations of a one-dimensional operation might have clarified the consequences of committing to such an operation and might have dispelled the notion that the threat of bombing or a few days of actual air strikes would cause Milosevic to back down.

The one-dimensional approach hampered the operation in other ways. For example, U.S. military doctrine outlines the command structure of joint task forces, including the designation of component commanders for land, maritime, and air forces. However, a land component commander was never designated for U.S. Joint Task Force Noble Anvil, the force that became the parent unit of the Army's Task Force Hawk. This absence complicated planning and day-to-day coordination. Furthermore, it took until late in the operation to achieve well-integrated joint targeting. Air Force targeters do not (and should not) have the expertise to plan attacks against ground forces. The Army and Marine Corps have this expertise, but in the absence of a joint targeting structure it was difficult to apply. Eventually the problem was solved, but not until late in the conflict.

One consequence of not having a true joint operation remains speculative: poorly developed ground operations. Because ground forces were rejected early in the decision process, no serious, comprehensive planning for their use took place. Some national staffs undertook a series of informal "assessments," but they lacked the comprehensiveness and coordination that effective plans require. Had Milosevic decided to weather the storm of air attacks longer than he did, the absence of joint planning almost certainly would have delayed an allied ground attack operation, pushing it into the winter or delaying it until the following spring, both bad options for the allies.

The operation also uncovered a gap in joint procedures: use of attack helicopters without ground forces. U.S. doctrine provides for attack helicopters to carry out deep strikes, but typically these occur as a combined arms team that includes ground maneuver forces. When Task Force Hawk deployed, established procedures did not exist for employing attack helicopters for deep strike in conjunction with air operations and without ground forces. Procedures were developed over time, but because the helicopters were never employed, the procedures were never tested. Joint doctrine was also not followed, in that supported and supporting command relationships were not established. In light of these experiences, then existing joint doctrine and tactics, techniques, and procedures (TTPs) were not well developed for the circumstances encountered. Therefore, there is a need for the Army and Air Force to develop more robust procedures for using attack helicopters in an air-only operation.

OTHER COORDINATION ISSUES

The lack of proficiency at employing joint procedures created one set of problems; additional discontinuities created others. One was a fundamental disagreement between the commander in chief (CINC) and his Air Component Commander about how to prosecute the air war. The former saw Yugoslav ground forces as a key center of gravity and the ultimate guarantor of Milosevic's power, and he wanted to attack them. The latter, recognizing the difficulty of doing serious damage to ground forces, judged attack of fixed targets as the best way to pressure Milosevic. Eventually, General Wesley Clark, NATO's Supreme Allied Commander Europe (SACEUR) as well as the U.S. European Command (USEUCOM) Commander, ordered Lieutenant General Michael Short, Commander, Allied Air Forces Southern Europe, to direct more attacks against ground force targets, but the differing philosophies remained a source of tension throughout the operation.

Task Force Hawk was also a contentious issue, but here the tension was between the CINC and the services, primarily the Army. Under U.S. procedures, the military services provide the forces the regional CINC determines he needs to carry out the mission given him by the National Command Authority. Thus, when General Clark requested an attack helicopter force, he expected the Army to provide it. But the Army leadership was skeptical of using helicopters in this specific situation, and all four services disagreed with the request when it was staffed through the Joint Staff. Eventually, the National Command Authority acceded to the CINC's request and authorized the deployment—but not the employment—of Task Force Hawk.

These sorts of discontinuities in military operations are not rare; indeed, they occur routinely. That an Army officer had a different view from an Air Force officer on the best way to prosecute an air operation or that a CINC disagreed with the Joint Staff about what he needed will surprise no one. What makes these differences noteworthy is their relevance to future operations. The United States can expect to find itself involved in future operations that will raise the same sorts of issues. Addressing them now will not only speed coordination in the future, but should also result in more effective operations.

RECOMMENDATIONS

The report makes a number of recommendations in the final chapter. Key among them are the following:

- A land component commander (LCC) should be routinely designated in joint operations against enemy land forces, whether or not sizable U.S. land forces are expected to be deployed in combat. The LCC is an essential advisor to the Joint Force Commander and can facilitate access to Army and Marine Corps targeting and planning assets and competence.

- In the case of striking fielded forces, the link between the sensors detecting the targets, the controllers authorizing strikes against those targets, and the shooters firing on the targets has too many parts and takes too long to be effective against such fleeting targets. A joint counterland control center should be established to speed this process and provide dynamic control of sensors and shooters.

- A contingency analysis cell should be established in the Army to aid the Army Chief of Staff, as a member of the Joint Chief of Staff, and CINCs in identifying and assessing land force options during crises and conflicts. This is particularly important in unanticipated situations where current plans do not exist or are inadequate.

- The Army needs to develop more expeditionary options below the corps level. Task Force Hawk exemplifies the kind of modularity the Army may need to offer to be most relevant in future operations. Smaller, more responsive, and more flexible force options must be part of the Army's overall inventory.

.

ACKNOWLEDGMENTS

Many people contributed to this report. Without their willing cooperation, the work could not have been completed. Research on operations reflected in this report was conducted by our colleagues John Bondanella, Richard Brennan, John Halliday, Richard Kedzior, and Deborah Peetz. For their continuous support, we thank our Army co-sponsors: Mr. Vernon Bettencourt, Technical Advisor to the DCSOPS, MG Robert St. Onge, Jr., and MG John R. Wood, Director, Strategy, Plans, and Policy (DCSOPS); Dr. Robin Buckelew, Director, Center for Land Warfare; and BG Lynn Hartsell, Director, Army QDR Office (DCSPRO). We also thank our points of contact with the sponsors for their support and access throughout this effort: Ms. Gail Lankford (Office of the Technical Advisor), LTC Robert Everson (Strategy, Plans, and Policy), and Mr. Timothy Muchmore (Center for Land Warfare/Army QDR Office). Jacqueline Henningsen, Director of Air Force Models and Simulation, assisted in securing Mission Analysis Tracking and Tabulation data from the Air Force's Warrior Preparation Center in Germany. We also gratefully acknowledge the support, guidance, and substantive contributions of David Kassing, director of the Strategy, Doctrine, and Resources Program in the Arroyo Center. RAND colleagues Lynn Davis, Paul Davis, Tom McNaugher, and Alan Vick all provided thoughtful and incisive reviews during the course of this research, as did Richard H. Sinnreich. Jerry Sollinger's organizational and editorial skills substantially improved and sharpened the final report. Special thanks to Regina Wright for her care and patience in the preparation of this document and to Joanna Alberdeston and Karen Echeverri for adding the finishing touches. We would also like to recognize the contributions of our RAND colleagues Kathy Mills, Jennifer Casey,

Gail Kouril, and MAJ Steve Perry, an Army Fellow. Also of RAND, Laurent Murawiec provided insightful comments on aspects of the NATO operations.

Finally, the report could not be realized without the invaluable assistance of many individuals involved in Operation Allied Force who provided information and in many cases interviews. These individuals are listed in the appendix.

ABCCC	Airborne Battlefield Command and Control Center
ACC	Air Component Commander
AFAC	Airborne Forward Air Controller
AFOR	Albanian Forces
AFSOUTH	Allied Forces Southern Europe
APC	Army Personnel Carrier
ARRC	Allied Command Europe Rapid Reaction Corps
ATACMS	Army Tactical Missile System
BCE	Battlefield Coordination Element
CAOC	Combined Air Operations Center
CBU	Cluster Bomb Unit
CRG	Contingency Response Group
CINC	Commander in Chief
DOCC	Deep Operations Coordination Cell
FLIR	Forward-Looking Infrared Radar
JSOTF	Joint Special Operations Task Force
JTF	Joint Task Force
KFOR	Kosovo Force

KLA	Kosovo Liberation Army
MEU	Marine Expeditionary Unit
MLRS	Multiple Launch Rocket System
MNB	Multi-National Brigade
MOG	Maximum on Ground
MUP	*Ministarstvo Unutrasnjih Poslova* (Ministry of the Interior)
NATO	North Atlantic Treaty Organization
NCA	National Command Authority
OSCE	Organization for Security and Cooperation in Europe
ROE	Rules of Engagement
SACEUR	Supreme Allied Commander Europe
SHAPE	Supreme Headquarters Allied Powers Europe
SOCEUR	Special Operations Command Europe
TF	Task Force
TLAM	Tomahawk Land Attack Missile
U.K.	United Kingdom
U.S.	United States
UAE	United Arab Emirates
UAV	Unmanned aerial vehicle
UN	United Nations
UNHCR	United Nations High Commissioner for Refugees
UNMIK	United Nations Interim Administration in Kosovo
UNSCR	UN Security Council Resolution
USA	U.S. Army
USAREUR	U.S. Army Europe

USAF	U.S. Air Force
USAFE	U.S. Air Forces in Europe
USEUCOM	U.S. European Command
USN	U.S. Navy
USNAVEUR	U.S. Navy, Europe
VJ	*Vojska Jugoslavije* (Yugoslav Army)

Chapter One

INTRODUCTION

The Kosovo conflict was unique in the history of the North Atlantic Treaty Organization (NATO). For the first time, the alliance conducted an offensive military operation to compel another country to accept its terms. For 78 days NATO waged a conflict under extremely demanding political and military conditions, ultimately forcing Yugoslavia to end Serb violence against the Kosovars, withdraw all Yugoslav forces from Kosovo, accept an international military presence in the province, and allow the unconditional return of all refugees. With the end of hostilities, NATO moved the Kosovo Force (KFOR) into Kosovo to establish basic law and order and provide protection for the people of Kosovo, a key NATO objective. In forcing Belgrade to accept its terms, NATO also demonstrated the alliance's resolve and ability to hold together in the face of many divisive pressures. The alliance accomplished all of this without committing ground forces to combat and without suffering any combat fatalities. By these many measures, Operation Allied Force can indeed be deemed a major success.

Yet NATO's use of force in dealing with Belgrade also revealed serious problems. What was to be a quick military operation instead became a 78-day campaign during which hundreds of thousands of Kosovars were displaced and thousands killed. One of the primary reasons for initiating military operations—to stop and deter further ethnic cleansing—was achieved in the end but at great cost to the Albanian Kosovars. NATO also set itself an objective to reduce the capability of Serb military forces to wage violence in the future. This too turned out to be a largely unmet goal, as Serb fielded forces survived NATO's air war largely intact. Finally, on the eve of Slobodan

Milosevic's capitulation, U.S. and NATO decisionmakers faced the imminent prospect of having to conduct a ground invasion for which detailed military planning and preparations were still quite limited. A decision to commit to a ground invasion of the Federal Republic of Yugoslavia would have severely tested NATO's political resolve.

A BATTLE OF CONSTRAINTS AND NATO'S STRATEGIC CHOICES

The conflict in Kosovo was the latest act in Yugoslavia's decade-long process of dissolution. Following repeated efforts in 1998 and early 1999 to reach a diplomatic settlement to halt Belgrade's repression of the Albanian Kosovars, on March 24, 1999, NATO set out to use limited air and missile strikes against Yugoslavia to compel it to accept a negotiated solution to the Kosovo crisis. NATO undertook Operation Allied Force with the widespread expectation that a relatively short bombing effort would quickly lead Serbian leader Milosevic to accept NATO's terms. It prepared for little more. When a rapid capitulation failed to materialize, NATO confronted not only an intransigent Serbian leadership but also the acceleration of a large-scale and ruthless displacement of Kosovars that NATO's original military action sought to prevent. Furthermore, during the coming months it would face constant political pressure both internally and from the larger international community to conduct a military campaign that kept NATO military casualties to a minimum; that minimized any collateral damage to civilians (Serbs and Albanian Kosovars alike); that restricted attacks on Yugoslav infrastructure; and that rapidly halted the ongoing ethnic cleansing.

These multiple objectives were in clear tension with one another and were, in many ways, contradictory. NATO's military operation during those 78 days was shaped by the need to pursue all the objectives throughout the course of the conflict. This had profound consequences for planning, for execution of the air operation, and for the deployment and employment of the U.S. Army's Task Force (TF) Hawk.

IMPACT ON PLANNING

Once the initial effort to quickly compel Milosevic failed, NATO faced the prospect of a protracted campaign. Yet little political foundation was laid for a sustained conflict, nor had there been any significant military planning for such a prospect. Many of the decisions leading to this situation had been made over the previous year. Well before Operation Allied Force began, U.S. and NATO senior civilian and military leaders had largely eliminated any prospect of using ground forces as part of an integrated campaign to meet NATO's objectives in Kosovo. The political and military costs and risks of conducting a ground operation were viewed as excessive, and there was no sense that an air-land operation was either appropriate or necessary. Therefore, from mid-1998 onward, not only was this option shelved, no serious contingency planning for air-land operations was undertaken. The exclusive planning focus was on air and missile strikes. NATO's military planning therefore evolved in a politically sustainable but militarily disjointed fashion.

In 1998 and early 1999, NATO did plan air operations that included "phases" permitting attack of targets beyond the initial strikes aimed at Yugoslavia's air defense system. These included possible attacks on ground forces in Kosovo (Phase Two), as well as attacks against hostile ground forces throughout the Federal Republic of Yugoslavia if necessary (Phase Three). But the emphasis was clearly on limited strikes to bring Milosevic back to the negotiating table, not on a long-term bombing campaign. The phases themselves became a means for exerting tight political control over any decision to escalate. Furthermore, the early elimination of planning for air-land operations meant that if anything beyond limited strikes were required, the phased air operation planning already had serious flaws built into it. While NATO could certainly hit fixed military targets, Serb fielded forces in Kosovo (NATO's Phase Two and Phase Three targets) were operating as dispersed battle groups. With the missions of combating the Kosovo Liberation Army (KLA) and terrorizing Albanian Kosovars, it was not necessary for Serb forces to concentrate. More important, facing no near-term prospect of a land invasion by NATO, these forces had no reason to concentrate and make themselves more lucrative targets for NATO air attack. When combined with the rugged terrain, poor weather, the need to keep NATO aircraft outside the range of air defenses, and the intermingling of civilians and hostile military units on the ground, NATO's subsequent air "phases" against the fielded forces had little prospect of military success.

In the case of U.S. air planning, a more robust air operation was in fact developed in the months prior to Allied Force. This planning focused on striking a much larger array of targets to include Yugoslav infrastructure. But this remained an air-only planning effort and not an integrated joint air-land approach. It did not focus on the Serb fielded forces as targets.

Finally, in the days just before Operation Allied Force, General Clark and others suggested the use of U.S. Army attack helicopters as another possible strike asset. But at the time the idea remained vague, with only the beginnings of a specified operational concept as part of any larger air operation planning. And precisely because any use of a ground maneuver force had already been ruled out at the time, exactly how attack helicopters would be employed as part of a phased air operation soon would raise controversial tactical and operational questions. Largely unaddressed and certainly unresolved before the conflict, these issues would contribute to the difficulties later encountered by TF Hawk once Allied Force was under way.

IMPACT ON AIR OPERATIONS

Expecting a short conflict that would bring Milosevic around, the North Atlantic Council approved only the first phase of the planned air operation at the outset of hostilities. Launched on March 24, this effort focused on a relatively small set of integrated air defense (IAD) and command and control targets. Available NATO air assets and targeting capabilities reflected the expectation of a short campaign. Following the first three days of Allied Force, Belgrade dug in, used its air defenses selectively to minimize NATO effectiveness, and launched its accelerated campaign of ethnic cleansing in Kosovo. NATO capitals were now under great political pressure to do something about the ethnic cleansing and end the mounting human tragedy. NATO expanded its air operations to include strikes against Yugoslav military (VJ) and Ministry of the Interior (MUP) forces in

Kosovo,[1] but these targets remained dispersed in difficult terrain, frequently located close to civilians and protected by still functioning air defenses. The absence of any joint air-land targeting capability in the early weeks of the conflict added to the difficulty. This absence was in large part driven by the expectation of a short campaign and the lack of planning for the integration of ground and air assets in this fashion to strike mobile fielded forces. The result was a largely ineffective air power effort against these forces. Of the large number of total strike sorties flown by NATO during Operation Allied Force, a relatively small percentage actually dropped weapons on these targets. Of these sorties, a significantly smaller percentage actually damaged or destroyed Serb equipment. And throughout this effort the number of Kosovar refugees mounted dramatically in the face of continuing VJ and MUP operations.

NATO's air effort against fixed military and infrastructure targets was far more successful. But even here, command and control and various air defense assets survived the bombing in relatively good shape, despite being priority targets. Over time, as it became clear that greater pressure was needed to coerce Belgrade, the scope and type of targets expanded significantly. But the approval process for this was often contentious and laborious, due in great measure to the political concerns of various alliance members. Yet despite these constraints, NATO's air operation against fixed targets ultimately brought great pressure to bear on the Belgrade leadership.

IMPACT ON TASK FORCE HAWK

Faced with Belgrade's continuing defiance and the flood of refugees, General Clark sought additional military options for putting pressure on Belgrade to stop the accelerated ethnic cleansing. One of these was his request for U.S. Army Apache attack helicopters. The concept was to have them positioned close to Kosovo where they would be used in conjunction with the ongoing air operation to strike at Serb forces in Kosovo.

From the outset the request for the Apaches was controversial among senior military officers in the United States. Several factors

---

[1]VJ is *Vojska Jugoslavije*; MUP is *Ministarstvo Unutrasnjih Poslova*.

were responsible, but central were concerns about the vulnerability of the Apaches to Serb low-altitude air defenses, the risk of striking internally displaced Kosovars while suppressing Serb air defenses, and the lack of lucrative targets given the dispersed nature of the enemy forces. It was also viewed by some as a nontraditional or "nondoctrinal" use of attack helicopters given the absence of a maneuver ground force, no designation of a land component commander, and the employment of the Apaches exclusively in support of an air operation. That these concerns were first raised after Operation Allied Force was under way was another manifestation of the disjointed approach to the conflict, specifically the lack of earlier joint force integration. Compounding the difficulties was the relatively compressed time in which viable operational concepts and an appropriate task force structure had to be developed. The composition of the task force was further complicated by a last-minute shift from a proposed deployment site in Macedonia to Tirana, Albania. This shift had major implications for force protection and engineering requirements that significantly increased the size of the task force. Confronting sharp differences of opinion among his senior military advisors, the President agreed to deploy the Apaches but withheld final approval for their employment.

Despite much popular criticism and official misstatements at the time on when the force would arrive, TF Hawk did, in fact, meet the designated deployment timeline of General Clark and the U.S. National Security Council. It did so in the face of several deployment challenges, most notably the highly constrained and congested airfield at Rinas that also served as the air hub for ongoing humanitarian relief operations. Once in Albania, additional time was required before TF Hawk was declared fully operational for deep-strike missions. Several factors were again responsible, but the dearth of pre–Allied Force joint planning for such contingencies was a contributing factor. There were problems integrating the helicopters into the ongoing air operation on the one hand, and integrating Army expertise and capabilities to support fixed-wing strikes on the other.

THE DEFICIENCIES OF OPERATION ALLIED FORCE

Allied Force demonstrated the strategic deficiencies of not taking a joint air-land approach to military operations. The political impediments to such an approach were real enough, but so too were the consequences of adopting a lesser strategy. In the run-up to Allied Force, Milosevic and his military commanders never confronted a credible threat of an air-land campaign. This probably encouraged Milosevic to conclude that NATO was not willing to take decisive military action and that he could outlast NATO's limited military efforts and political resolve. Once Allied Force began, the continuing absence of a credible air-land option ceded the initiative to Belgrade. The Serbs responded with an accelerated ethnic cleansing campaign that NATO had little ability to stop or even deter in any military sense. NATO's only near-term option was an expanded air operation. Limited to this, the alliance could not impose the demanding synergies of an air-land threat on Serb fielded forces. Consequently those forces could—and did—remain dispersed, significantly reducing the effectiveness of air strikes while allowing Serb units to continue apace with their ethnic cleansing. As a result, in the test of wills Belgrade might well have concluded it had a serious chance of bringing the most pressure to bear, outlasting NATO and achieving a strategic victory. The fact that Milosevic greatly miscalculated the unifying effect that his ethnic cleansing would have on NATO's resolve does not diminish the fundamental point: the adversary was not presented with a robust array of interlocking military threats that either would compel acceptance of NATO's terms or lead to the rapid destruction of Serb military forces.

Beyond the strategic argument, the absence of a joint air-land approach also contributed to operational and tactical deficiencies in executing even the phased air campaign adopted by NATO. Outside of some preliminary exploration by General Clark on the use of attack helicopters, pre–Allied Force air planning did not consider Army assets that could have improved the effectiveness of the phased air campaign in Kosovo. Attack helicopters, short- and long-range rocket and missile fires, and the host of target development and location identification capabilities of the U.S. Army against deployed enemy fielded forces were not integrated into early air planning. Doing so might well have improved the effectiveness of air strikes against even dispersed targets in Kosovo earlier in the conflict. Furthermore, the lack of prior joint air-land planning contributed to delays and uncertainties by senior commanders as to how exactly the task force was to be used and what it brought to the fight. The absence of a land component commander contributed to these short-falls in early integration. Therefore, the failure to treat the conflict as a joint operation from the outset meant that air-land synergies were not fully exploited even within the restrictive confines of an "air only" campaign.

The report that follows examines these issues in detail. It looks at the operational history of Allied Force, its success and failures, and the reasoning and decisions behind various aspects of the military operation. It then explores the implications of this experience for the future, particularly in terms of the Army's role in joint and multinational operations as part of its ongoing transformation. It concludes with a series of recommendations for the Army and for future U.S. joint and multinational operations.

ABOUT THE REPORT

This report exploits open sources but has the advantage of building on research conducted using classified sources through SECRET level. Inevitably, it omits much material, especially concerning tactics and weapons performance, that would enrich and deepen the analysis. However, enough material has become publicly available to support a reasonably detailed account of events.

Information for this project came from five sources. First, Arroyo Center analysts had access to a large number of the military planning and operation documents of significance. These included concept plans, operation plans and orders, and other documents pertaining to the planning and execution of the military operations carried out in and around the Balkans. Second, the team was given a host of material pertaining to the actual conduct of the operations. These materials included such things as air tasking orders, situation reports, intelligence summaries, battle damage assessment reports, command briefings, and deployment data. Third, the team received a number of reports written about the conflict. These included after action reports from military units and NATO allies and the very substantial report to Congress by the Department of Defense. Many of the unclassified materials collected for this study are unpublished and therefore are not available to the public. Citations are made accordingly. Fourth, the team visited a number of sites in Europe and the United States, including all the major commands; the defense ministries of France, Germany, and the United Kingdom; the Pentagon; the U.S. Central Intelligence Agency; the U.S. Defense Intelligence Agency; and the National Ground Intelligence Center. During these visits, we interviewed dozens of participants, including many senior officers. The experiences, observations, and insights of these participants were an invaluable complement to written records. The authors are most grateful for their willingness to discuss events and share information. Many of these interviews were conducted on a "nonattribution" basis. As a result, we do not identify individuals when drawing on these interviews. The appendix lists the individuals with whom we met. The team was unable to interview senior members of the Joint Staff, Office of the Secretary of Defense, and, with few exceptions, members of the National Security Council. Finally, the team benefited greatly from other ongoing work in the Arroyo Center, Project AIR FORCE, and the National Security Research Division within RAND.

Chapter Two

AT THE BRINK: APRIL 1998 TO MARCH 1999

Military planning in the twelve months before Operation Allied Force was driven by NATO's limited political objectives—and the corresponding limited means it was willing to use—in dealing with the Kosovo crisis. The objective was to dampen the escalating hostilities by both the Serbs and the KLA in order to stop the mounting human suffering and to prevent the violence from spreading to neighboring countries. Of primary concern was the danger of spillover to Macedonia and Albania, as well as to the Yugoslav territory of Montenegro, risking larger Balkan instability. From the outset, NATO and the United Nations pursued these objectives through a mix of diplomatic incentives and threats. The overwhelming desire was for a diplomatic settlement in which military forces would be used to implement a diplomatic solution, not impose a violent one. To the extent military force was to be used as a stick, it was construed largely in terms of a limited coercive use to compel Belgrade to accept a negotiated solution.

The genesis of Operation Allied Force also took place within a larger context of NATO air operations in the former Yugoslavia extending back to 1993. Throughout this period, the United States promoted the use of air power, usually against Serbs, whom Washington regarded as the most aggressive party. Air power was the force of choice because it minimized risk to friendly forces, typically produced highly discriminate effects, and could be turned on and off at will.

Limited coercion by air power had worked before. Most dramatically, from August 29 to September 20 in 1995, NATO conducted Op-

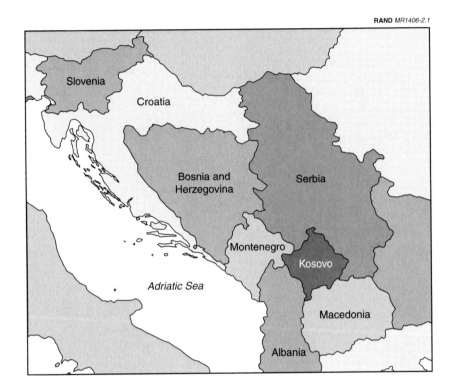

Figure 2.1—Map of the Balkan Region

eration Deliberate Force. The principal goals were to end attacks by Bosnian Serb forces on "safe areas" and to ensure withdrawal of Serb heavy weapons from an exclusion zone around Sarajevo. During the operation, NATO flew 3,315 sorties, of which 2,285 (65 percent) were flown by U.S. aircraft. Strike aircraft were directed to fly above the range of low-level air defenses, and none were lost. Milosevic did in fact capitulate, although a major contributing factor was the ongoing ground operations undertaken by Croatian forces. Therefore a pattern of diplomacy backed by the coercive use of air power already existed as the 1998–1999 crisis in Kosovo escalated.

MOUNTING TENSIONS AND CONCERNS OVER KOSOVO

After the Dayton accords of December 1995, the Federal Republic of Yugoslavia included Serbia and Montenegro. But a major outstanding issue was the future status of Kosovo. The Kosovar Albanians did not get a hoped-for restoration of their political rights following Dayton, sowing the seeds for the upcoming violence in the province.

On December 16, 1997, the North Atlantic Council[1] expressed concern over escalating ethnic tension in Kosovo and called upon the parties to find a mutually acceptable solution. On March 5, 1998, the council issued a statement of its "profound concern" over the escalating violence in Kosovo, condemning both the Yugoslav repression of ethnic Albanian political expression and the terrorism of the KLA. It called for negotiations to address ethnic Albanian concerns. It noted that "NATO and the international community have a legitimate interest in developments in Kosovo . . . because of their impact on the stability of the whole region."

On March 9, 1998, the Contact Group (high-level representatives of France, Germany, Italy, Russia, United Kingdom, and the United States) issued a statement condemning attacks by Yugoslav forces and called for immediate cessation of hostilities. The Contact Group also announced that it was considering punitive measures, including an arms embargo and economic sanctions. Growing involvement by the international community came with the March 31, 1998, United Nations Security Council Resolution 1160, condemning the excessive use of force by Yugoslav forces against Kosovar civilians. It also imposed an arms embargo on Yugoslavia.

Initial NATO Planning

Initial NATO planning for both potential ground and air operations began in April 1998. During April and May, the Supreme Allied

---

[1]The North Atlantic Treaty of 1949 established only one formal decisionmaking body: the North Atlantic Council. It meets at various levels. The permanent council is composed of ambassadors and meets at least weekly. Meetings at the level of foreign ministers and defense ministers take place at six-month intervals. There have been fifteen meetings at the level of heads of state and government, the most recent being the Washington Summit on April 23–24, 1999, to commemorate the alliance's 50th anniversary.

Commander Europe, General (USA) Wesley K. Clark, directed the commander of Allied Forces Southern Europe, Admiral (USN) James Ellis, to plan for a "preventive deployment" into Albania and Macedonia. These operations consisted of deploying NATO troops to these front-line states as a means to help stabilize them in the face of growing violence and political instability along their borders with Yugoslavia.[2]

Formal NATO planning for potential ground and air operations against Yugoslavia began in early June. Under this authority, Allied Forces Southern Europe started to plan for both permissive and opposed military intervention. On June 17, the North Atlantic Council asked the Military Committee to assess the full range of graduated options to deter further violence and to influence the behavior of the parties to the conflict.[3] These fell into two broad categories: planning for military peace operations as part of a negotiated settlement, and planning for offensive military combat operations—air and land—should they become necessary. In the case of offensive military operations, NATO planning quickly evolved in the direction of air and cruise missile strikes as the preferred method for coercing Belgrade.

Forced-entry ground operations were effectively ruled out by both senior NATO political authorities and U.S. political and senior military leaders by the summer of 1998. With the exception of some broad estimates on what types of forced-entry land operations might be considered and what they would require, neither NATO nor the United States planned for land invasion from June 1998 until after Operation Allied Force began in March 1999. Throughout these many months the focus was instead on limited, coercive uses of force to help bring about a political settlement of the Kosovo conflict.[4]

---

[2]Interviews with planners at Headquarters, Allied Forces Southern Europe, and cited in General Wesley K. Clark, *Waging Modern War* (New York: Public Affairs, 2001), p. 114.

[3]The day before, June 16, NATO signaled its possible use of military force over the deteriorating situation in Kosovo with a one-day air exercise in Albanian and Macedonian airspace, code-named Operation Determined Falcon.

[4]As General Clark put it with regard to NATO's military planning, "the whole purpose of the NATO effort was to empower diplomacy." Clark, *Waging Modern War*, p. 121.

This focus and planning approach produced a major "disjoint" in which air operations were now separated from an air-land campaign.

OCTOBER CRISIS

In the fall of 1998, Yugoslavia continued its brutal suppression of the KLA. On August 12, NATO Secretary General Javier Solana publicly blamed Milosevic for the violence and revealed that the North Atlantic Council had reviewed a range of military options. Presumably in an attempt to avert NATO action, President Milosevic announced on September 28 that the KLA had been defeated and Yugoslav forces would withdraw from Kosovo. But one day later, nineteen Kosovar Albanians were found massacred in Gornje Obrinje west of Pristina. On October 5, the UN Secretary-General Kofi Annan issued a report that condemned the killing and destruction by Yugoslav forces operating in Kosovo. The same day, U.S. envoy Richard Holbrooke, accompanied by an aide to the Supreme Allied Commander Europe, met with Milosevic to discuss the crisis. A television statement in Milosevic's name declared that Holbrooke had made "threats of aggression" and that NATO was supporting "Albanian terrorists."

During the October crisis, the North Atlantic Council took a variety of actions to back diplomacy with military force. Solana informed the press that the North Atlantic Council had directed preparation for limited air strikes and a phased air operation over Yugoslavia with execution in approximately 96 hours. On October 12, U.S. National Security Advisor Samuel L. Berger said that NATO was ready to conduct air strikes against Yugoslavia to assure compliance with NATO demands. However, he added: "I don't think that the American people will support ground troops, U.S. ground troops in Kosovo."[5] The following day, Holbrooke and Milosevic announced agreement on a plan to end the conflict in Kosovo. This plan included reduction of Yugoslav forces in Kosovo, deployment of 2,000 unarmed inspectors, and NATO aerial surveillance of the province. On October 15, Solana and General Clark met Milosevic in Belgrade and an agreement was signed with the Yugoslav Chief of the General Staff con-

---

[5]R. Jeffrey Smith, "Accord on Kosovo Remains Elusive," *Washington Post*, October 12, 1998, pp. A14, A22.

cerning aerial surveillance. The North Atlantic Council also approved the Kosovo Verification Mission Agreement with Yugoslavia, the unarmed observers charged with monitoring the situation in Kosovo.

The United States and other members of the Contact Group and NATO were eager to support the Holbrooke-Milosevic agreement and the nascent Kosovo Verification Mission operation. Two supporting peace operations resulted: Operation Eagle Eye, the air verification mission over Kosovo, and Operation Determined Guarantor, a force to protect the Kosovo Verification Mission.

Operation Eagle Eye provided air surveillance to verify compliance by all parties in the region with the provisions of the October agreement. The three critical tasks in Eagle Eye were verification, assessment, and reporting. Films and images from Eagle Eye's manned and unmanned surveillance platforms were delivered to NATO processing stations. An analysis of the NATO-collected information was conducted at NATO, and this assessment was shared with the Kosovo Verification Mission, led by the Organization for Security and Cooperation in Europe (OSCE), and with the UN.[6] The overall objective was to provide NATO headquarters a clear picture of the situation in Kosovo. Surveillance flights continued from November 1998 until March 1999. Operation Eagle Eye ended with the launching of Operation Allied Force. Likewise, when the Yugoslav government failed to comply with the Holbrooke-Milosevic agreement by continuing to build up its military forces, it placed the Kosovo Verification Mission at risk. The mission was withdrawn and Operation Joint Guarantor was canceled in the days just prior to Allied Force.

In retrospect, the October crisis had several important consequences. It brought NATO to the brink of executing a limited air strike and kept this option permanently on the table. It led to deployment of the Kosovo Verification Mission under the auspices of the OSCE, opening a window on Yugoslav oppression of the Kosovar Albanians. And it led to deployment of surveillance aircraft over Kosovo, allowing NATO planners to gain familiarity with the terrain. Finally, and perhaps most significantly, it suggested that Milosevic

---

[6]See *http://www.afsouth.nato.int/operations/deteagle/Eagle.htm*.

would back down when threatened with air strikes, encouraging NATO to make this threat again.[7]

RAMBOUILLET AND ITS AFTERMATH

Despite repeated warnings from NATO and the Contact Group, Yugoslav forces continued a campaign of repression in Kosovo. On January 15, 1999, Yugoslav security forces massacred some 45 Kosovo Albanians near the village of Racak. The following day, on January 30, the North Atlantic Council demanded that those responsible be brought to justice and threatened air strikes. On February 16, Milosevic announced that he would not allow foreign troops to enforce an agreement. Three days later, the U.K. 4th Armored Brigade and elements of the Allied Command Europe Rapid Reaction Corps headquarters began deployment through Greece to Macedonia.[8] On the same day, Solana announced that NATO was willing to lead a peacekeeping force in Kosovo and would take whatever actions were necessary, including air strikes, to avert a humanitarian catastrophe.

In mid-February 1999, Yugoslav negotiators and representatives of the Kosovar Albanians met at Rambouillet Chateau near Paris in a conference co-chaired by representatives of France and the United Kingdom. The parties negotiated over an Interim Agreement for Peace and Self-Government in Kosovo, known as the Rambouillet Accords. These accords would have affirmed the territorial integrity of the Federal Republic of Yugoslavia, but they provided that after three years an international meeting would be convened to determine a mechanism for final settlement of the Kosovo problem. Yugoslavia would have withdrawn its army forces from Kosovo, withdrawn Ministry of the Interior units from Kosovo not assigned there prior to February 1, 1998, and withdrawn air defense forces beyond a

---

[7]As General Clark summarized the October crisis, "This was diplomacy backed by threat. The air threat helped to halt the Serb campaign in Kosovo, just as I had expected. Milosevic was intimidated by NATO air power, even in the absence of a significant ground threat." Clark, *Waging Modern War*, p. 153.

[8]Macedonia was one of six constituent republics of the former Republic of Yugoslavia. When it became independent, Greece strongly opposed the use of the name "Macedonia" on historical grounds. Macedonia is therefore officially known as the Former Republic of Macedonia (FYROM).

25-kilometer Mutual Safety Zone. NATO would have led a military force to ensure compliance.[9]

On February 23, the Rambouillet conference adjourned without agreement despite personal mediation by U.S. Secretary of State Madeleine K. Albright. The talks resumed in Paris on March 15, but ended three days later when the Yugoslav negotiators refused to sign. Particularly onerous for Milosevic and the Yugoslavs were the provisions allowing NATO peacekeeping forces access throughout the Federal Republic and references to ultimate self-governance for Kosovo. On March 18, international mediators held a one-sided signing ceremony for the Kosovar Albanian delegation.

Secretary General Solana reiterated NATO's willingness to use whatever means necessary to bring about a peaceful solution and avert a humanitarian crisis. In a news conference on March 19, President Clinton said, "If we do not act, the war will spread." The following day, the Kosovo Verification Mission withdrew from Kosovo, as urgently recommended by NATO's Military Committee. On March 22, Holbrooke met with Milosevic in Belgrade in a last effort to persuade him to sign an interim peace plan. The next day, Holbrooke briefed the Secretary General on his failed effort in Belgrade. The North Atlantic Council noted that the Secretary General had consulted with all members of the alliance and had decided to begin air strikes in Yugoslavia. Solana directed General Clark to initiate air strikes and then announced that NATO was acting because Yugoslavia refused to accept the interim peace agreement negotiated at Rambouillet, declined to hold Yugoslav forces in Kosovo to limits agreed upon in October, and continued to use excessive force.

NATO's limited phased air operations planning had changed little during the intervening months and remained the only politically agreed-upon response. Development of a more robust air campaign plan, code-named "Nimble Lion," had been under way in U.S.-only channels (primarily at U.S. Air Forces Europe, or USAFE), but it was regarded by General Clark as too large and unrestricted to gain NATO

---

[9]United Nations Security Council, letter dated June 4, 1999, from the Permanent Representative of France to the United Nations, addressed to the Secretary-General, enclosing the Rambouillet Accords: *Interim Agreement for Peace and Self-Government in Kosovo*, S/1999/648, June 7, 1999.

approval.[10] NATO instead continually reviewed lesser air options and never developed a full air campaign. Forced-entry ground options remained beyond consideration.[11] At higher levels, there seems to have been general expectation that President Milosevic would capitulate under threat of air attack or after a few days of bombing. As one history observed, "NATO did not expect a long war. Worse, it did not even prepare for the possibility."[12] The die was cast as NATO set out to initiate Phase One of its air operation on March 24. It did so not only without a serious military alternative, but also with virtually no attention to integrating elements of a land force into the NATO air campaign. This was soon to have important operational consequences.

---

[10]General Clark states that the U.S. air plan was briefed to NATO in July 1998, where it was met with resistance as being "too large, too threatening." NATO authorities wanted more limited options. One result was the creation of a so-called Limited Air Option, consisting only of cruise missile strikes against a small number of targets, with no manned aircraft. Clark, *Waging Modern War*, pp. 124–125. Also, interviews conducted by the authors at NATO Headquarters, November 1999.

[11]According to General Clark, both he and Klaus Naumann (Chairman of the NATO Military Committee) raised the need for developing a ground option with Secretary General Solana, but were told by him that the NATO nations were not prepared to take on the issue at the time. Clark adds that "if we pushed too hard for an immediate commitment to go in on the ground, we jeopardized our ability to take action at all." Clark, *Waging Modern War*, pp. 166–167.

[12]Ivo H. Daalder and Michael E. O'Hanlon, *Winning Ugly: NATO's War to Save Kosovo*, Washington, D.C.: Brookings Institution Press, 2000, p. 103.

Chapter Three

AIR OPERATION

Western leadership expectations for a brief bombing effort and rapid capitulation by Milosevic were instead met with Belgrade's defiance. The regime severed diplomatic relations with Western powers and accelerated its "ethnic cleansing" of Kosovar Albanians. The test of political and military wills now began in earnest.[1]

NATO AND U.S. GOALS

Official NATO and U.S. statements announced the same goal in undertaking the air operation against Yugoslavia: to stop the violence against Kosovar Albanians.

Just before NATO air strikes, NATO announced that its military action was "directed towards disrupting the violent attacks being committed by the Yugoslav army and Special Police Forces and weakening their ability to cause further humanitarian catastrophe."[2] The Secretary General stated: "We must stop the violence and bring

---

[1] In his account, General Clark states that in a meeting with Secretary of State Albright a few weeks prior to Operation Allied Force, he explained that it was almost certain that Belgrade would attack civilian Kosovars and that there was little NATO could do about it. "Despite our best efforts the civilians are going to be targeted by the Serbs. It will just be a race, our air strikes and the damage we cause them against what they can do on the ground. But in the short term, they can win the race." Clark, *Waging Modern War*, p. 171.

[2] NATO Press Statement (1999)040, March 23, 1999.

an end to the humanitarian catastrophe now taking place in Kosovo."[3]

Also just prior to NATO air strikes, the U.S. Department of Defense announced: "The primary goal of air strikes, should Secretary General Solana make that decision, would be to arrest the ability of the Serbs to brutally attack the Kosovar Albanians."[4] In an initial public statement, President Clinton outlined similar objectives:

> Our strikes have three objectives: First to demonstrate the seriousness of NATO's opposition to aggression and its support for peace. Second, to deter President Milosevic from continuing and escalating his attacks on helpless civilians by imposing a price for those attacks. And third, if necessary, to damage Yugoslavia's capacity to wage war against Kosovo in the future by seriously diminishing its military capabilities.[5]

PUBLIC RENUNCIATION OF GROUND FORCE OPTIONS

In Washington, the Administration was reluctant to consider the use of ground forces, believing that there would be inadequate political support. Indeed, the United States had been reluctant to contribute ground troops even to a postconflict peace operation. On the eve of the air campaign, the United States finally agreed to participate in a peace operation, but demanded the sector it considered easiest to handle.[6]

Speaking on March 24 in the Oval Office, President Clinton said: "If NATO is invited to do so, our troops should take part in that mission to keep the peace. But I do not intend to put our troops in Kosovo to

---

[3]NATO Press Statement (1999)041, Statement by Secretary General Dr. Javier Solana, March 24, 1999.

[4]Department of Defense News Briefing, Statement by Assistant Secretary of Defense for Public Affairs Kenneth Bacon, Washington, D.C., March 23, 1999.

[5]Statement by President William Jefferson Clinton, White House Briefing Room, Washington, D.C., March 24, 1999.

[6]Wesley K. Clark, "Risking the Alliance," *The Washington Post*, December 8, 2000, p. A41.

fight a war."[7] Subsequently, in an interview broadcast on national news, he was asked to clarify his position on ground troops in Kosovo and replied that "the thing that bothers me about introducing ground troops into a hostile situation—into Kosovo and the Balkans—is the prospect of never being able to get them out."[8]

At the Pentagon, Department of Defense spokesman Kenneth Bacon stated on March 27 that "The United States has no intention of sending ground troops to fight in Kosovo, and the Department of Defense is not doing any planning that would enable such a deployment."[9] These statements might well have encouraged Milosevic to hold out, implying that he might prevail if he could endure air attacks, themselves limited by NATO's own goals and inhibitions.

National Security Advisor Berger subsequently defended these public statements, eschewing the use of ground forces as essential to keeping the alliance together on Kosovo. Referring to President Clinton's March 24 statement of having no intention of introducing ground troops, Berger remarked that "we would not have won the war without this sentence."[10] In addition, Berger was convinced that Congress would not approve funding for any operations involving ground forces. Concerns over a possible land invasion were so severe that even after it was clear the initial bombing had failed to compel Belgrade, no formal military contingency planning for a possible invasion occurred. Rather, a series of largely unconnected "assessments" by small planning cells was all that took place. This would remain the case well into the air operation. Whatever the political merits of resisting any ground operation planning, it did have serious military consequences.

---

[7]Statement by President William Jefferson Clinton, White House Briefing Room, Washington, D.C., March 24, 1999.

[8]Interview of the President by Dan Rather, Columbia Broadcasting System, The White House, Washington, D.C., March 31, 1999.

[9]Assistant Secretary of Defense Kenneth H. Bacon, Pentagon, Washington, D.C., March 27, 1999.

[10]Cited in Daalder and O'Hanlon, *Winning Ugly*, p. 97.

INITIAL OPERATIONS

NATO initiated Operation Allied Force with 214 U.S. aircraft (not counting B-2s operating from the continental United States) and 130 aircraft from twelve other members of the alliance.[11]   The alliance also had naval assets positioned within cruise missile range of Yugoslavia, including four U.S. surface ships, two U.S. attack submarines, and a British attack submarine. However, the United States had no large-deck carrier available. A few days earlier, the USS *Theodore Roosevelt* carrier battle group had left the Mediterranean on its way to the Red Sea in response to building tensions with Iraq, making it unavailable until April 6, about two weeks into the operation.

The operation began during the night of March 24, with cruise missile attacks primarily against Yugoslav air defenses. The United States fired Tomahawk Land Attack Missiles (TLAM) from four surface ships and two submarines in the Adriatic, while the United Kingdom fired land attack missiles from the attack submarine HMS *Splendid*. The next wave of missiles consisted of AGM-86C conventional air-launched cruise missiles (CALCM), fired from B-52 bombers from outside Yugoslav airspace and directed mainly at Yugoslav command and control facilities, air defense sites, and airfields. Fifty-one targets were included in the initial strike plan.[12]

During the first night, most of the Yugoslav MiG-29s took off, and some attempted to engage NATO aircraft. U.S. F-15C fighters downed two MiG-29s, and a Dutch F-16 fighter downed another. There were no friendly losses. During the second night, two MiG-29s apparently tried to intercept a U.S. KC-135 tanker but were downed by U.S. F-15C fighters. In future operations, Yugoslav aircraft occasionally tried to infiltrate NATO flights but never mounted significant opposition. During the first night, Yugoslav air defense forces left their acquisition radars off and did not attempt to engage NATO aircraft. But subsequently, Yugoslav forces began to blink their acqui-

---

[11]Department of Defense, *Report to Congress, Kosovo/Operation Allied Force After Action Report*, Washington, D.C., January 31, 2000, p. 31.

[12]As General Clark describes it, this initial operation combined the Limited Air Option (missile strikes) with Phase One of the NATO phased air operation (the use of manned aircraft primarily to strike against Yugoslavia's air defense system). Clark, *Waging Modern War*, p. 176.

sition radars in attempts to engage NATO aircraft without presenting good targets for anti-radiation missiles.

General Clark defined three military "measures of merit" that guided the conduct of the air operation. The first was minimizing the loss of friendly aircraft. The second was "impacting Serb military and police in Kosovo." The third was minimizing collateral damage. A fourth, political, measure of merit related to these other three was to maintain alliance cohesion throughout the operation.[13]

Command and Control

Operation Allied Force was conducted through both NATO and U.S. command channels. The overall commander was General Clark, serving as both Supreme Allied Commander Europe (SACEUR) and Commander-in-Chief, U.S. European Command (USEUCOM). Clark's U.S. air component commander was General (USAF) John P. Jumper, serving as Commander, USAFE. The NATO operational commander was Admiral (USN) James O. Ellis, serving as Commander, Allied Forces Southern Europe; Commander-in-Chief, U.S. Naval Forces Europe; and Commander, Joint Task Force Noble Anvil.[14] His headquarters was in Naples, Italy. Subordinate to Ellis was Lieutenant General (USAF) Michael C. Short, Commander, Allied Air Forces Southern Europe; and Commander, U.S. 16th Air Force, with headquarters in Aviano, Italy. U.S. air assets were committed to Operation Allied Force in three ways: General Jumper had operational control of B-1, B-2, B-52, F-117, E-3C, KC-135, and reconnaissance aircraft, while giving tactical control to General Short. General Short had operational control over other aircraft, organized into the 31st Air Expeditionary Wing headquartered at Aviano, the 16th Air Expeditionary Wing also headquartered at Aviano, and the 100th Air Expeditionary Wing headquartered at Mildenhall, United Kingdom.[15] Finally, the Joint Special Operations Task Force controlled U.S. and

---

[13]Clark, *Waging Modern War*, p. 346.

[14]Joint Task Force Noble Anvil controlled the U.S. component of Operation Allied Force.

[15]The Air Force is in the process of creating Air Expeditionary Forces. Although these were unavailable for Operation Allied Force, the concept was exercised.

NATO aircraft dedicated to combat search and rescue (see Figure 3.1 for the locations of these commands).

NATO countries gave operational or tactical control over their forces to Admiral Ellis as the operational NATO commander. The following NATO allies contributed forces: Belgium, Canada, Czech Republic, Denmark, France, Germany, Greece, Hungary, Iceland, Italy, Luxembourg, Netherlands, Norway, Poland, Spain, Turkey, United Kingdom, and the United States. Admiral Ellis directed air missions for conventional aircraft through a NATO-releasable air tasking order

RAND MR1406–3.1

Figure 3.1—Command Headquarters Locations

prepared in the Combined Air Operations Center (CAOC) in Vicenza, Italy. In addition, 16th Air Force prepared a U.S.-only air tasking order for U.S. stealth aircraft.

Restrictions on Air Operations

At the start of operations, only a small number of targets had been approved for strike. An array of authorities, including those at the highest national political levels, permanent representatives on the North Atlantic Council, Supreme Allied Commander Europe, air planners in Allied Forces Southern Europe, and authorities in countries hosting NATO aircraft were involved in the target-approval process. The risk of collateral damage was always an important consideration in deliberations over targets.

Since the alliance's primary goal was to compel Yugoslav forces to end violence against the Kosovar Albanians, it could not afford to be seen as acting inhumanely, as applied to both Kosovar Albanians and Serb civilians. The rules of engagement were therefore highly restrictive, reflecting NATO's goals and moral values. They required positive identification of targets before pilots were cleared to release ordnance. Moreover, forces were not allowed to attack military vehicles if they were intermingled with civilian vehicles.[16]

YUGOSLAV FORCES

Yugoslavia proved resourceful at using its mostly older-generation air defense weapons to maintain an enduring air defense threat to NATO aircraft. Emphasizing long-term survival in the face of overwhelming air power, enough surface-to-air missiles and anti-aircraft cannon survived to pose a constant low- and mid-altitude threat to

---

[16]As one participant noted, "At the Combined Air Operations Center during the conflict, because we were so concerned with collateral damage, General Short put out the guidance that if military vehicles were intermingled with civilian vehicles, they were not to be attacked due to collateral damage. At the same time, the Serbs had cover of weather. . . . Therefore another ROE [rules of engagement] position would happen that unless you could clearly identify the target, you were not to drop." General (USA) Wesley K. Clark and Brigadier General (USAF) John D. W. Corley, press conference on the Kosovo strike assessment, Headquarters, Supreme Allied Command Europe, Mons, Belgium, September 16, 1999.

NATO aircraft. By forcing aircraft to largely remain at or above 15,000 feet, it magnified NATO's difficulties in conducting effective strike operations by exploiting the alliance's highly restrictive rules of engagement and need for "eyes on target" to avoid civilian casualties. In so doing, Yugoslavia made the most of a very weak air-defense hand. Likewise, when it came to its fielded forces Yugoslavia made good use of dispersion and terrain to minimize the effectiveness of NATO air strikes. Even before Operation Allied Force began, Yugoslav ground forces in Kosovo were operating in small unit formations, making them difficult targets for air attack.

Air Defense

Yugoslavia had older air defense weapons of Soviet design cued by newer, commercially available radars and coordinated through redundant communications, including landlines. All told, Yugoslavia shot down only two NATO aircraft, but its air defenses survived and presented a nearly constant threat. The risk was so great at low altitude that General Short initially ordered his pilots to stay at medium or above altitude (15,000 feet), where only SA-6 missiles could reach them.

The SA-6 (NATO designation "Gainful") system was the most modern large surface-to-air missile in Yugoslavia's inventory. The system mounts three missiles on a lightly armored, tracked vehicle. The missiles are equipped with semi-active radar homing and a folding antenna for the Straight Flush radar. The basic system can engage to an altitude of about 42,000 feet. An SA-6 crew would normally keep its radar off until cued through an early-warning system that an aircraft was within range. In Russian practice, one or more SA-6 systems would normally fire two or three missiles per engagement to increase the probability of kill. During Operation Allied Force, Yugoslav SA-6 gunners faced a dilemma. If they completed a radar-guided engagement, NATO aircraft would have time to respond with anti-radiation missiles. But if they used radar sporadically, even a spray of missiles would be unlikely to down an aircraft. In most instances Yugoslav gunners opted for safety, using their radars only sporadically and accepting low effectiveness.

In Kosovo, the Yugoslav army presumably deployed the low-level air defense assets organic to its ground units. The M53/59 twin 30mm cannon has a maximum horizontal range of 9,700 meters (31,816 feet), a maximum vertical range of 6,300 meters (20,664 feet), and an effective anti-aircraft range of 3,000 meters (9,840 feet). The gunners must rely on visual identification, and they have no night-vision equipment. The M55 is a triple 20mm cannon normally towed by a truck. The M75 is a single 20mm cannon on a light carriage, which may be towed or disassembled and man-packed. The BOV-3 features a triple 20mm cannon in an open-topped turret on a lightly armored wheeled vehicle. It has infrared night-vision equipment. Its maximum vertical range is 2,000 meters (6,560 feet), but the effective anti-aircraft range is probably 1,000–1,500 meters (3,280–4,920 feet). The SA-7 is a man-portable heat-seeking missile with a 1.15-kilogram fragmentation warhead effective to an altitude of about 1,500 meters (4,920 feet) against approaching jet aircraft and 1,800 meters (5,904 feet) against jet aircraft going away. However, earlier versions of the SA-7 tend to lose lock when fired head-on and are much more effective in tail-chase mode. The SA-9 (NATO designation "Gaskin") has four missiles mounted on a lightly armored wheeled vehicle. These missiles have more advanced, all-aspect heat-seekers effective to an altitude of 3,500 meters (11,480 feet). Taken together, these weapons posed a dangerous and unpredictable low-level threat.

Yugoslavia also had some fifteen new MiG-29 (NATO codename "Fulcrum") and sixty older MiG-21 (NATO codename "Fishbed") fighters. But their pilots were at a hopeless disadvantage against their NATO opponents.

Suppression of Yugoslav air defense was an endless task. EA-6B Prowler aircraft and F-16CJ routinely supported air strikes. The Yugoslav air defenders chose to limit emissions, thereby surviving, but as a result shot down only two NATO aircraft. On March 27, a Yugoslav surface-to-air missile downed a U.S. F-117 Nighthawk Stealth fighter about thirty miles northeast of Belgrade. According to a senior U.S. defense official, the aircraft had descended below cloud cover to deliver weapons and was then tracked by electro-optical means.[17]

---

[17]William B. Scott, "Pentagon Mum About F-117 Loss," *Aviation Week & Space Technology*, April 5, 1999, p. 31.

NATO forces never completely suppressed the opposing anti-aircraft missiles, but they did make these missiles ineffective by making full radar guidance too risky for the Yugoslav operators. Typically, the operators would fire shots of three missiles at the approximate altitude and track of an aircraft, hoping that a warhead would detonate within lethal radius of the target. In this mode, they fired hundreds of missiles while downing only two aircraft. When their radar-warning gear alerted pilots that a launch was in progress, they took successful evasive action, essentially turning at faster rates than the approaching missile. On the other hand, U.S. pilots were frustrated in their efforts to destroy mobile SA-6 systems because they either could not engage them quickly enough or could not find them in Kosovo's rough terrain.[18]

Ground Forces in Kosovo

The Yugoslav army had been operating in small combined arms "battle groups" since the spring of 1998. To protect and assist the counterinsurgency (and later, ethnic cleansing) activities of the Ministry of Interior forces, the Yugoslav army divided its forces into these company- and battalion-sized organizations. Typically, a company-sized battle group would consist of a company of motorized infantry, a platoon or two of tanks, half a battery of artillery and/or heavy mortars, a few engineers and logistics troops, and a small amount of air defense such as a platoon of anti-aircraft guns (usually 20mm or 30mm automatic weapons that were normally employed in a ground attack mode against the KLA). Throughout the fall of 1998 and into early 1999 the Yugoslav army operated in this manner, giving junior leaders months of experience in dispersed, combined arms operations before NATO's air attacks began. This dispersed mode of operations was ideal for minimizing the effect of those air attacks once Operation Allied Force started.

---

[18]For a detailed discussion of the challenges NATO encountered in suppressing Yugoslavian air defenses, see Benjamin S. Lambeth, *"NATO's Air War for Kosovo,"* Santa Monica, CA: RAND, MR-1365-AF, 2001, especially pp. 102–116.

SLOWLY EXPANDING AIR OPERATIONS

NATO cautiously and incrementally expanded the allowable target sets in Yugoslavia. General Clark insisted on greater apportionment of air effort against Yugoslav forces in Kosovo, despite General Short's misgivings. Finally, General Clark received very strong reinforcement for the air effort from the North Atlantic Council.

Introduction of Naval Air

Much to the consternation of Admiral Ellis, the United States initiated Operation Allied Force without any aircraft carriers within range. Indeed, the USS *Theodore Roosevelt* battle group had been ordered to proceed to the Persian Gulf area. But when Belgrade refused to capitulate quickly, the *Roosevelt* was ordered back to the Adriatic Sea. Its sorties flew almost exclusively into Kosovo and usually against Yugoslav forces. Carrier-based aircraft normally flew as complete strike packages, including F-14 and F-18 for strike, EA-6B for suppression of air defenses, F-14s as airborne forward air controllers, and E-2C as airborne control centers. E-2C aircraft normally conduct radar surveillance, but during Operation Allied Force they provided an interface between the CAOC in Vicenza and assets in the area of operations, including strike packages and intelligence collectors.[19]

On April 15, *Roosevelt* aircraft struck Podgorica air base in Montenegro. Montenegro was largely exempted from air attack because its government was at odds with the Belgrade regime, but Podgorica air base was an exception. Aircraft based there could attack TF Hawk forces deploying to Albania. During a videoteleconference, General Clark ordered Vice Admiral Daniel J. Murphy, Jr., Commander, U.S. Sixth Fleet, to attack Podgorica. The strike was carried out the same afternoon.[20]

---

[19]Commander Wayne D. Sharer (USN), "The Navy War Over Kosovo," *Proceedings*, October 1999, pp. 26–29; Robert Wall, "E-2Cs Become Battle Managers with Reduced AEW Role," *Aviation Week & Space Technology*, May 10, 1999, p. 38.

[20]Vice Admiral (USN) Daniel J. Murphy, Jr., "The Navy in the Balkans," *Air Force Magazine*, December 1999, p. 49.

Expansion of Fixed Targets

On March 28, after protracted discussions, the North Atlantic Council authorized attacks against a broader range of fixed targets throughout Serbia proper and also to escalate attacks on Yugoslav forces in Kosovo, which were accelerating the cleansing of ethnic Albanians.[21]   During this discussion, General Klaus Naumann of Germany, Chairman of NATO's Military Committee, reportedly argued that NATO should start "attacking both ends of the snake by hitting the head and cutting off the tail."[22] Attacking the head of the snake implied hitting targets throughout Serbia, especially those most closely associated with the regime's sources of authority. On April 1, NATO began to strike infrastructure in Serbia, including a major bridge over the Danube River at Novi Sad, but no targets in the immediate Belgrade area. On April 12, NATO struck the oil refinery at Pancevo and oil storage facilities.

Aircraft Reinforcement

On April 9, General Clark asked for an additional 82 U.S. aircraft and on April 13 another 300 U.S. aircraft, bringing the total number of requested aircraft to about 800. The plan for U.S. reinforcement of Operation Allied Force was dubbed "Papa Bear" because it was the largest of three options under consideration. Admiral Ellis and General Short advised Clark against Papa Bear on the grounds that they had neither adequate basing nor enough approved targets. Indeed, Short ultimately concluded that about half the targets approved for strikes were of questionable value.[23] Despite this advice, General Clark pushed ahead with Papa Bear, wanting to send a strong signal to Milosevic of the growing U.S. air power that could be used against

---

[21]General Clark reported that during the first few days of the air operation, "We were striking at the facilities of the Serb ground forces that were doing the ethnic cleansing, but we hadn't yet struck those forces." Clark, *Waging Modern War,* p. 211.

[22]William Drozdiak, "NATO Leaders Struggle to Find a Winning Strategy," *Washington Post,* April 1, 1999.

[23]USAFE interview of Lieutenant General Michael C. Short, Commander, Allied Air Forces Southern Europe, and Commander, 16th Air Force, interview file reviewed at Studies and Analysis, U.S. Air Forces in Europe, Einsiedlerhof, Germany. Short characterized the less-worthwhile targets as "stop signs and fire hydrants."

him.[24] Papa Bear arrived in increments throughout Operation Allied Force and was not yet fully deployed when the operation ended. By the end, NATO could have generated about 1,000 sorties per day but actually generated many fewer, primarily due to a lack of suitable targets and poor weather on some days. Nevertheless, the large influx of aircraft may have influenced Milosevic's decision to end the conflict.

The United States conducted about two-thirds of all sorties, while undertaking most of the effort in the key functions of reconnaissance, suppression of air defenses, and strike with precision-guided munitions. Within the U.S. effort, U.S. Air Forces flew most of the sorties into Yugoslav airspace, operating from bases in Germany, Italy, the United Kingdom, and Turkey. U.S. Navy aircraft operated from the USS *Theodore Roosevelt* in the Adriatic Sea and Aviano (EA-6B aircraft), while the U.S. Marine Corps flew from Taszar, Hungary (F/A-18D aircraft). B-2 missions originated from their home base at Whiteman Air Force Base, Missouri.

Controversy Over the Weight of Effort

Following the NATO decision to intensify attacks on Yugoslav forces in Kosovo, General Clark directed General Short to apportion more sorties to these attacks. Clark believed that destruction of these forces would help convince the Yugoslav leaders to yield and end the conflict. He considered the Serb ground forces to be a "center of gravity" for Milosevic and, as such, that the Serb leader could ill afford to have those forces seriously damaged.[25] Moreover, he was keenly aware of political pressure to show results against these forces. NATO much preferred to attack forces that were conducting "ethnic cleansing" than to punish Serbs generally. The allies hoped eventually to bring Yugoslavia into the European family of nations and therefore did not want to impoverish the country or to embitter its citizens. NATO may also have anticipated that the European Community might have to shoulder part of the burden of recon-

---

[24]General Clark states in his account that beyond intensifying the air campaign, he also wanted the additional aircraft in place for a potential ground option. Clark, *Waging Modern War,* p. 265.

[25]Interviews with authors, and in Clark, *Waging Modern War,* pp. 241–242.

structing Yugoslavia after the conflict ended, another argument for minimizing attacks on infrastructure.

In contrast, General Short preferred to concentrate air power against fixed targets in Yugoslavia. Short believed that "We could not stop the killing in Kosovo from the air . . . . We were not going to be efficient or effective."[26] If the Yugoslav leaders attacked the Kosovar Albanians, then air power should be directed against leadership targets in Belgrade.[27] In Short's opinion, it made more sense to attack the head of the snake in Belgrade than the tail in Kosovo. Moreover, he anticipated that air power would not be very effective against forces dispersed throughout Kosovo's rugged terrain. General John P. Jumper, Commander, U.S. Air Forces Europe, held the same opinion. Jumper said: "No airman ever promised that air power would stop the genocide that was already ongoing by the time we were allowed to start this campaign."[28] Clark finally ordered Short to apportion more sorties against Yugoslav army and police forces operating in Kosovo.

For lack of a more appropriate term, the U.S. Air Force usually called attacks on Yugoslav forces in Kosovo "close air support," although there were no friendly ground forces to support.[29] Aircraft providing "close air support" flew at least 15,000 feet above ground level until Commander Allied Air Forces Southern Europe or his representative gave approval to expend ordnance and the strike aircraft was handed off to a tactical air control party or airborne forward air controller. Normally, aircraft within what was designated the Kosovo Engagement Zone used standard procedures for "close air support." An EC-130E/J Airborne Battlefield Command and Control Center

---

[26]See General (USAF) Michael E. Ryan, *The Air War over Serbia*, Studies and Analysis Directorate, United States Air Force in Europe, Ramstein Air Force Base, Germany, 2000, p. 19.

[27]USAFE interview of General Short, op. cit.

[28]Ibid.

[29]Close air support is defined as "air action by fixed- and rotary-wing aircraft against hostile targets which are in close proximity to friendly forces and which require detailed integration of each air mission with the fire and movement of those forces." See *DoD Dictionary of Military and Associated Terms*, Washington, D.C.: Joint Publication 1-02, Joint Chiefs of Staff, 2000, and *Joint Tactics, Techniques, and Procedures for Close Air Support (CAS)*, Washington, D.C.: Joint Pub 3-09.3, Joint Chiefs of Staff, 1995, p. I-1.

would designate areas within Kosovo for attack using a grid system. As strike aircraft entered Kosovo airspace, typically just after refueling, they would contact the EC-130E/J for instructions. Controllers on the EC-130E/J would brief the pilots and hand them off to forward air controllers, usually flying OA-10A aircraft. The EC-130 would also provide updated intelligence to the forward air controllers, who would then direct their strike aircraft to their targets, assuring themselves that the pilots had correctly identified the aim points. The basic links are depicted in Figure 3.2.

NATO employed a variety of munitions against Yugoslav forces, including the Maverick, laser-guided bombs, cluster bombs, and general-purpose gravity bombs. Each of these munitions had advantages and disadvantages. Maverick was designed to destroy armored vehicles using television, infrared, or laser guidance. It offered high

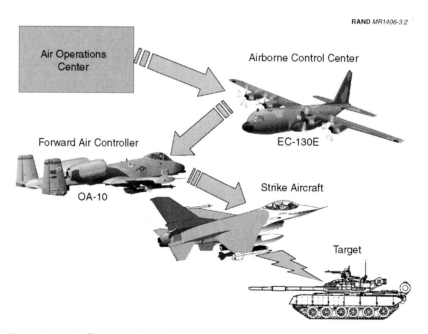

RAND *MR1406-3.2*

Images courtesy Department of Defense.

Figure 3.2—Basic Process for Attacking Fielded Forces

lethality, once the missile locked on the target, and low risk of collateral damage. Cluster munitions, such as the U.S. Cluster Bomb Unit (CBU)-87 and the British BL-755, provided area coverage using bomblets.[30] But these highly effective munitions also posed high risk of collateral damage if the target were misidentified or civilians were in the vicinity. They also posed the longer-term dangers of remaining unexploded bomblets once hostilities ceased. Less accurate general-purpose bombs could be highly effective when used in large numbers, but the risk of collateral damage constrained their use.

NATO'S DETERMINATION TO PREVAIL

As the conflict wore on and Belgrade continued its killing and displacing of Kosovars, NATO faced mounting pressure to halt the ethnic violence and to end the conflict on terms acceptable to NATO. In the face of continued defiance from Belgrade, the alliance now had to bring greater pressure to bear on the Yugoslav leadership while preserving NATO's unity.

Turning Point: The NATO Summit Conference

On April 23–24, NATO held a summit meeting in Washington, D.C., to commemorate the 50th anniversary of its founding.[31] The NATO leaders naturally devoted much attention to Kosovo—NATO's first and to-date only offensive combat operation. At the time, Operation Allied Force appeared far from a success. U.S. National Security Advisor Samuel Berger subsequently said that these leaders unanimously agreed: "We will not lose. Whatever it takes, we will not

---

[30]CBU-87 dispenses 202 bomblets in a rectangular pattern, the size of which depends on release parameters and the spin rate of the dispenser. It is described as a combined-effects munition because the bomblets variously employ shaped charge, fragmentation, and incendiary devices. The bomblets are exploded by a proximity sensor at predetermined heights.

[31]The North Atlantic Treaty was signed in Washington on April 4, 1949, creating an alliance of ten European and two North American (Canada and the United States) countries committed to collective self-defense. With the admission of the Czech Republic, Hungary, and Poland on March 12, 1999, the alliance expanded to nineteen members.

lose."[32] According to the statement issued by the heads of state and government,

> The crisis in Kosovo represents a fundamental challenge to the values for which NATO has stood since its foundation: democracy, human rights and the rule of law. It is the culmination of a deliberate policy of oppression, ethnic cleansing and violence pursued by the Belgrade regime under the direction of President Milosevic. We will not allow this campaign of terror to succeed. NATO is determined to prevail.[33]

In the same statement, the NATO leaders made five demands on President Milosevic: "Ensure a verifiable stop to all military action and the immediate ending of violence and repression in Kosovo"; withdraw military, police, and paramilitary forces from Kosovo; allow the stationing in Kosovo of "an international military presence," understood to imply NATO forces; allow the safe return of refugees; and work toward an agreement "based on the Rambouillet accords."[34]

Escalating Attacks on Yugoslav Infrastructure

As noted, even before the summit NATO expanded its target sets in Yugoslavia. On April 21, two days before the summit, NATO attacked the official radio and television station in Belgrade with cruise missiles. The station went off the air for several hours but then resumed operation, eliciting another attack. Although NATO gave warning of the attack, sixteen people working in the building were killed. NATO argued that these attacks were justified because the station was an organ of official propaganda. The Milosevic regime did indeed use the official radio and television stations to propagate its policies while it censored and harassed independent senders. However, some commentators, including Amnesty International, believed that attacking the television station constituted a violation of the laws of

---

[32]Doyle McManus, "Clinton's Massive Ground Invasion That Almost Was," *Los Angeles Times*, June 9, 2000.

[33]Heads of state and government participating in the meeting of the North Atlantic Council in Washington, D.C., April 23–24, 1999, *Statement on Kosovo*, NATO Press Release S-1(99)62, Washington, D.C., April 23, 1999.

[34]Ibid.

war.[35] On the same day, NATO destroyed the last remaining bridge over the Danube at Novi Sad, ironically a city whose municipal government opposed the Milosevic regime.

At the time of the Washington summit conference, NATO began attacking electric power transformers. The United States advocated more extensive attacks on electrical power generation, but other NATO members, especially France, counseled restraint. To address the French concerns, the United States offered to use CBU-94, a then-secret cluster bomb that ejects large numbers of fine carbon-graphite threads. These threads short-circuit electrical lines, causing outage until they can be removed. On May 3, F-117s dropped CBU-94 on transformers in five locations, temporarily disrupting electrical power in most of Serbia. During what proved to be the last two weeks of the air operation, NATO finally began to attack power generation energetically. During May 24–26, NATO aircraft struck electrical power facilities in Serbia's three largest cities (Belgrade, Novi Sad, and Nis), leaving most of Serbia without electrical power for days. Although these attacks were ostensibly aimed against military use of electrical power, they likely had greater effect on the civilian economy. Military users were more likely to have backup generators, especially to support vital functions such as communications with deployed forces.

Halting Steps Toward a Possible Land Invasion

Once it became apparent that the Yugoslavs were not going to bow quickly to NATO's demands, NATO started to reconsider the prospect of a forced-entry ground operation. But that prospect remained highly undesirable and politically charged. This was reflected in the approach taken toward military planning for a land invasion. The North Atlantic Council did not authorize planning for such a possibility, and the United States continued to reject the option of ground operations. Under these restrictive political conditions, U.S. and NATO military planners were not authorized to conduct traditional campaign planning. What emerged in its place came

---

[35]See Amnesty International, *"Collateral Damage" or Unlawful Killings? Violations of the Laws of War by NATO during Operation Allied Force,* London, England, June 7, 2000.

to be known as military "assessments." By this device, military planners could consider various ground options in the absence of specified authority to do so. More than a semantic difference, these "assessments" tended to be compartmentalized within specific organizations, often limited in their detail, and could not be coordinated and integrated with operational units, service force providers, transportation providers, and all of the other organizations involved in traditional campaign planning. Most were undertaken by very small planning staffs with extremely restricted ability to reach beyond those staffs for necessary information and additional planning expertise.

According to General Clark's account, he raised the issue of planning for a ground option in an April 9 meeting with Secretary General Solana and General Naumann. Solana reportedly supported exploring options as long as it could be done discreetly. A few days later on April 13, General Clark had a videoteleconference with the U.S. Joint Chiefs of Staff and Secretary of Defense Cohen, in which Clark described the need to proceed with planning and preparations for a ground option.[36]

A series of "assessments" were undertaken at U.S. Army Europe, U.S. European Command, Joint Task Force Noble Anvil, V Corps, and Headquarters Department of the Army. These activities were reported to be of varying levels of depth, but often they were fairly generic and lacked many of the details routinely associated with integrated campaign planning. Because the "assessments" fell outside of both NATO and U.S. political channels, they also lacked any specified political guidance on objectives and constraints. And again the planning was largely confined to the organizations themselves.[37]

General Clark's planning cell continued to refine ground options throughout April and May, with a strong emphasis on an attack into Kosovo from Macedonia and Albania. The invasion would be limited to Kosovo itself. General Clark estimated that to conduct a decisive operation to secure Kosovo in a few weeks, he would need six divi-

---

[36]Clark, *Waging Modern War,* pp. 252, 254.

[37]Multiple interviews with planners and senior military officials.

sions consisting of light, heavy, and mixed forces (about 175,000 total troops).[38]

In late May, the Joint Chiefs of Staff met with the President to discuss the status of Operation Allied Force. Toward the end of the meeting the issue of ground operations was discussed. General (USA) Dennis J. Reimer, the Army Chief of Staff, expressed his view that if forced-entry ground operations were to be used, the center of gravity for addressing the larger Balkan problem was Belgrade. This meant a much larger operation, attacking not primarily from the poor infra-structure of Albania, but through Bulgaria and Hungary. Such a large ground operation would require a near-term decision (early June) to get everything in place before winter.[39] While many forced-entry assessments had been conducted up to this point, no integrated campaign planning was under way.

The British were also conducting unilateral assessments of the re-quirements for a ground offensive into Kosovo. The British were the strongest advocates of ground offensive operations within the al-liance. When it appeared that the air operation was not achieving rapid results, the British began to assess several courses of action for a ground offensive. A planning group in England provided recom-mendations and evaluations to the highest levels of the British gov-ernment. Although aware that the Americans were starting to exam-ine various options during April, the British planners had to conduct their assessments separately. The British expected that if NATO decided to conduct a ground attack, their assessments would be combined with similar American efforts to create a formal NATO operational plan.

By early June, then, several independent efforts to develop ground offensive courses of action were under way at U.S. and British head-quarters. None of these efforts had progressed to the stage of a formal plan, and much more work would have been required to inte-grate schemes of maneuver with transportation and logistics plans. Nevertheless, American and British planners were developing op-tions for a ground offensive to begin in early or mid-September had

---

[38]Clark, *Waging Modern War,* pp. 301–302.

[39]Army interview, December 3, 1999.

air operations proved unsuccessful in forcing the government in Belgrade to comply with NATO's conditions.

On June 2, Berger held a discussion at the National Security Council with experts who had advocated use of land forces. Berger said that NATO was absolutely determined to prevail. He argued that the air operation was having a serious impact but added that the President had not ruled out other options. After this discussion, Berger composed a memorandum for President Clinton outlining three courses of action: (1) arming the Kosovar Albanians; (2) continuing the bombing and waiting until spring 2000 for a possible ground offensive; and (3) conducting a ground invasion in the fall of 1999. Arming the Albanians would lead to decades of conflict, and waiting until spring would mean a miserable winter for thousands of internally displaced persons. NATO could open a corridor to assure these people safe exit from Kosovo, but the military requirement would be about the same as for an invasion. Berger concluded that invasion would be the only viable option if Belgrade remained intransigent.[40] Before Operation Allied Force ended, President Clinton appears to have been on the verge of a decision to conduct an invasion, with the United States making the largest contribution. However, Clark was still restricted to conducting informal planning only and to begin improving roads through Albania to the Kosovo border.

Although U.S. and British "planning" for a possible ground offensive was not complete at the time Operation Allied Force ended, it is likely that the gradual increase in preparation for a ground option influenced Milosevic's decision to end the conflict. By late May, media reports about the increased likelihood of a ground attack were becoming more frequent. The presence of the U.S. Army's TF Hawk in Albania could logically be interpreted in Belgrade as the nucleus for a much larger NATO ground force, and, of course, major elements of NATO's Allied Command Europe Rapid Reaction Corps were already in Macedonia. The increased probability of an eventual NATO ground offensive probably contributed to Belgrade's decision to end hostilities.[41]

---

[40]Daalder and O'Hanlon, *Winning Ugly,* pp. 158–160.

[41]How much of a role a potential ground invasion played in Belgrade's final decision to capitulate to NATO's demands will most likely never be known. While arguing that

It is unclear whether the North Atlantic Council would have approved a ground invasion and which members would have participated, either within the alliance or as a coalition of the willing. Greek public opinion strongly opposed the air effort and would likely have been vehemently against a ground invasion. Even so, the Greek government would probably have allowed use of its seaports because the NATO alliance is central to its security policy. Italian public opinion divided about evenly, and its administration openly disagreed on the question. However, the prime minister and the defense minister both indicated that Italy would contribute to a ground invasion if NATO decided to conduct one. Germany was in a more difficult position. Public opinion was evenly divided, and Foreign Minister Joschka Fischer had barely managed to maintain support from his Green Party for the air operation. At the Washington summit, Chancellor Gerhard Schröder openly opposed a ground invasion, and it is at least doubtful whether his Socialist-Green government would have approved German participation. Britain, under the leadership of Prime Minister Anthony Blair, strongly advocated a ground invasion, especially in bilateral talks with the Americans. The British planned to contribute a very large contingent, necessitating a large callup of its Territorial Army.[42] Finally, it is uncertain how the U.S. Congress and public would have reacted to a ground invasion.

---

a combination of factors were at work, in *Winning Ugly* authors Ivo Daalder and Michael O'Hanlon state that the threat of a ground war "was a critical factor in Milosevic's thinking . . . and it is doubtful that the war could have been won without it" (p. 203). Another assessment of Milosevic's reasons for settling acknowledges the contribution of a possible ground invasion, but argues that the dominant military factor influencing Belgrade's decision was the prospect of an intensifying air campaign against infrastructure targets. A third study gives more weight to the building evidence of a possible land invasion in the closing days of Operation Allied Force, but maintains that air power—and the prospects of its continued use and escalation—created many of the key conditions necessary for an eventual political settlement. And there were of course the changing political conditions, including growing political pressure from Russia on Belgrade to reach a settlement. The latter two studies were done by RAND, the first by Stephen T. Hosmer, *The Conflict Over Kosovo: Why Milosevic Decided to Settle When He Did*, Santa Monica, CA: RAND, MR-1351-AF, 2001, the second by Benjamin S. Lambeth, *NATO's Air War for Kosovo: A Strategic and Operational Assessment*, Santa Monica, CA: RAND, MR-1365-AF, 2001.

[42]Secretary of Defense Cohen met in late May 1999 with NATO defense ministers from Britain, France, Germany, and Italy to discuss steps for a possible land invasion. The meeting reportedly concluded that NATO governments now had to make a decision within days on whether to commit to a possible ground offensive and begin movement of troops. See Dana Priest, "A Decisive Battle That Never Was," *Washington Post*, September 19, 1999, p. A01.

The U.S. House of Representatives was sending mixed messages over the air operation, having refused to approve it while voting funds to continue it. In the end, Congress would probably have supported a determined President or at least not have denied funding.

Tightening the Noose: The Ahtisaari-Chernomyrdin Mission

The air effort against Yugoslavia put Russia in a difficult position. Russian public opinion and opinion within the Duma strongly opposed NATO's action, widely thought to be illegal and discriminatory against the Serbs. Russia opposed a Security Council resolution that would have legitimized the operation. But the Russian leadership was interested in good relations with the West, especially in view of its worsening economic problems. Therefore a ground invasion would have confronted the Russian leadership with highly unpleasant alternatives: do nothing and appear impotent, support NATO and outrage Russian opinion, or oppose NATO and risk losing invaluable assistance.

Beginning in late May 1999, U.S. Deputy Secretary of State Strobe Talbott (representing NATO), former Russian Premier Viktor Chernomyrdin, and Finnish President Martti Ahtisaari (representing the European Union) met several times to discuss conditions for ending the conflict. On May 27, while these negotiations were continuing, Chernomyrdin met with Milosevic. The Yugoslav leader insisted that countries that had participated in the air effort should not deploy peacekeeping forces to Kosovo, thus excluding all of NATO's prominent members. He also wanted Russia to occupy a northern sector where the Serb population is concentrated. The United States had already rejected this idea because it could lead to partition. During a dramatic final negotiating session in Bonn on June 1, the United States and Russia finally reached agreement on terms for ending the air operation. Ahtisaari and Chernomyrdin delivered these terms, which largely coincided with those announced at the NATO summit conference, to Milosevic in Belgrade on June 2. They told Milosevic that they had not come to negotiate, only to present terms. Confronted with this solid front, which included the only major power that might have sided with Yugoslavia, Milosevic capitulated.

NATO negotiated with Yugoslav military authorities over the terms for the withdrawal of Yugoslav forces from Kosovo. The Yugoslavs objected to a seven-day time limit, proposing instead fifteen days. They eventually received eleven days from the time of signing (June 9), which was more than fifteen days after Yugoslavia formally agreed to NATO's terms (June 3). The Yugoslav military also persuaded NATO to reduce the Ground Safety Zone on the Serb side of the border with Kosovo from 15 miles to 3 miles (5 kilometers). Even this much-reduced zone later became a sanctuary for Kosovar Albanian separatists, prompting strenuous Serbian protests.[43]

With the signing of the Military Technical Agreement on June 9, air operations were suspended, and NATO prepared to move into Kosovo to enforce the newly arrived-at agreement.

SUCCESSES AND LIMITATIONS OF THE OVERALL AIR OPERATION

NATO's bombing campaign was central to ultimately getting Belgrade to end hostilities on terms acceptable to NATO. Many other factors contributed to this successful outcome, but the daily and escalating bombing exerted great pressure on the Yugoslav leadership to relent. This was especially true as attacks on infrastructure mounted. Still, by relying on air power as the single military instrument, combined with the practical political-military restrictions imposed on its use, NATO discovered both the strengths and limits of air power as a coercive instrument.

NATO allies were reluctant to punish Yugoslav citizens for the policies of the Milosevic regime, and they did not want to impoverish or embitter Yugoslavia. Therefore, they approved only a gradually increasing and tightly constrained air effort to keep pressure on Belgrade. That effort had to find a delicate balance: enough destruction to coerce Milosevic, but not enough to dismay the NATO allies. At the same time, it had to avoid losses that could weaken domestic support. In addition to the political-military challenges this condition imposed, it placed NATO in a moral dilemma: rather than risk pilots' lives to protect innocents on the ground, NATO protected its pilots even though this increased the likelihood of additional civilian

---

[43]At this writing NATO has agreed to allow the Serbs to conduct armed patrols in response to increased Albanian paramilitary activities.

casualties, through less accurate bombing. This dilemma exerted political pressure during the conflict, but not enough to force NATO to back down before Milosevic agreed to accept its terms. In the end, NATO prevailed, and air power proved successful in many respects. But significant problems were revealed as well, especially against Serb military forces in Kosovo.

Overall Success

Despite incomplete planning and preparation, highly restrictive rules of engagement, and bad weather, NATO rapidly mounted an impressive air effort. It achieved air supremacy at middle and high altitudes while avoiding low-level air defenses. It lost only two aircraft to hostile fire, and both pilots were rescued. With few exceptions, NATO systems performed well in combat, and operational readiness rates were generally high. NATO expended over 20,000 weapons with few errors and caused relatively little collateral damage, notwithstanding some high-profile exceptions. NATO's success was largely due to U.S. air forces that flew two-thirds of all sorties and made key contributions in reconnaissance, air defense suppression, and all-weather precision strike. The B-2 bomber had an impressive combat debut.

Fixed Targets

Fixed targets included command, control, communications, and intelligence; Yugoslav army infrastructure; lines of communication; petroleum, oil, and lubricants; defense industry; and electric power. NATO dropped all three Danube bridges at Novi Sad, blocking river traffic, but left six Danube bridges at Belgrade (three highway, two railroad, one highway/railroad) intact. NATO destroyed rail lines leading into Kosovo and damaged roads in five main corridors.

NATO was highly successful against Yugoslavia's war-related and dual-use industry. It destroyed 40 percent of capacity to repair armored vehicles, half of capacity to produce explosives, 65 percent of capacity to produce ammunition, and 20 percent of capacity to assemble and repair aircraft.[44]

NATO attacked transformer stations and transmission towers in Yugoslavia proper, disrupting electrical power throughout Yugoslavia. Power went down in Belgrade and Novi Sad for extended periods and was frequently disrupted across wider areas.

Limited Collateral Damage

Minimizing collateral damage was vital to maintaining public support, especially in Europe. At the start of the air effort, important segments of European public opinion were ambivalent about or even opposed to bombing. Reservations were especially strong among Green members of the ruling coalition in Germany, many of whom had roots in the pacifist movement. In retrospect, perhaps the greatest risk to NATO policy was some catastrophic incident of collateral damage that might have swayed public opinion against the operation and compelled the alliance to stop bombing before its demands were met.

According to a thorough investigation undertaken by Human Rights Watch, approximately 500 Yugoslav civilians were killed in 90 separate incidents during Operation Allied Force.[45] These incidents peaked during the last days of May. Five of the ten worst incidents involved attacks on presumed convoys or transportation routes, including four incidents in Kosovo. Most collateral damage was slight and went largely unnoticed in the media. But some was spectacular and elicited widespread attention. Among these were the attacks on the Grdelica Klisura railway bridge that killed 20 passengers, the Djakovica-Decane road attack in which 73 civilians were killed, and most politically damaging, the inadvertent bombing of the Chinese Embassy in Belgrade on May 7. These episodes caused acute political problems and forced immediate adjustments in air operations.

---

[44]Interviews at U.S. European Command, November 12, 1999.

[45]William M. Arkin, "Civilian Deaths in the NATO Air Campaign," Human Rights Watch, *http://hrw.org/hrw/reports/2000/nato*. Human Rights Watch concluded that as few as 489 and as many as 528 Yugoslav civilians were killed in 90 incidents. Casualty estimates in the following paragraphs are drawn from Appendix A of the report, "Incidents Involving Civilian Deaths in Operation Allied Force."

But overall, NATO air operations inflicted remarkably little collateral damage given the number of strikes conducted.

Operational Problems

Despite its overall success, Operation Allied Force also revealed problems with the air operation. Although the United States suffered extremely low losses to air defenses, indeed fewer than expected, Operation Allied Force demonstrated that a moderately sophisticated integrated air defense system, when combined with highly restrictive rules of engagement, could severely constrain air operations. As the U.S. Air Force observed, "Had the Serbs been able to employ the latest generation of surface-to-air missiles and aircraft, air superiority would have been considerably more difficult to achieve."[46] More advanced shoulder-fired weapons would also have posed a greater threat to the Army's Apache helicopters.

One obvious problem was a widening gap in capabilities between U.S. and other NATO air forces. Superior U.S. performance made other NATO countries painfully aware that they had not kept pace with recent developments in air power. They lacked secure communications and information systems capable of handling large amounts of data. With few exceptions, they lacked precision-guided munitions, both all-weather such as Joint Direct Attack Munitions and clear-weather such as AGM-130. Moreover, despite fifty years of standardization efforts, NATO forces still exhibited significant interoperability problems. NATO heads of state launched a Defense Capabilities Initiative during the Washington Summit in April 1999 to improve defense capacity, but declining or stagnating European defense budgets could make some problems intractable.

Operation Allied Force also revealed challenges for U.S. air forces. It showed again that some high-demand assets might be largely or almost completely committed to a Kosovo-sized contingency, raising doubt whether U.S. air forces have the appropriate mix and number of assets to execute the national military strategy. These assets included RC-135 Rivet Joint aircraft collecting electronic intelligence, F-16CJ aircraft carrying High-Speed Anti-Radiation Missiles, and

---

[46]Ryan, *The Air War over Serbia*, p. X.

EA-6B aircraft equipped to jam enemy radars. It also indicated that work was needed to shorten the air tasking order cycle and to make the reconnaissance–assessment–strike link more responsive. And despite much technical progress, poor weather remained a serious impediment to air operations against many ground targets.[47] Finally, Operation Allied Force demonstrated that U.S. air forces could not inflict much damage on fielded forces if those forces dispersed and employed cover and concealment techniques in rugged terrain.

LOW EFFECTIVENESS OF AIR STRIKES AGAINST FIELDED FORCES

Fielded forces in Kosovo proved difficult to attack successfully for several reasons. Persistent cloud cover hampered reconnaissance and often prevented optical target acquisition. But even on clear days, the province's rugged and varied terrain offered many opportunities to conceal forces from air attack. Almost completely unchallenged on land, Yugoslav forces could disperse and hide under trees and in villages. When they did reveal themselves, slowness in the sensor–controller–shooter sequence often gave them enough time to relocate before air attacks. Rules of engagement were highly restrictive to minimize risk to Kosovar Albanians, the people that air strikes were intended to protect. Pilots had to identify their targets positively, which often proved impossible even when reconnaissance indicated that Yugoslav forces were almost certainly present in a given area. To avoid low-level air defenses, pilots were generally held at medium altitudes, further increasing the difficulty of target identification. Nor is it clear that pilots could have identified and tracked fielded forces in the rough Kosovo terrain, even had they flown at much lower levels. To solve this problem, high-resolution sensors, extensive data exploitation, and highly survivable or expendable reconnaissance platforms are needed. The inability to inflict signifi-

---

[47]The Balkans are noted for severe and violently changeable weather. During Operation Allied Force, poor weather proved to be a major impediment, especially to attacks on Yugoslav forces in Kosovo. There was 50–100 percent cloud cover 72 percent of the time, and only 21 of 78 days had good overall weather. In all, 3,766 planned sorties, including 1,029 sorties characterized as "close air support," were aborted due to weather. Not until late May did the weather become consistently favorable.

cant damage on Serb fielded forces had severe consequences for meeting key NATO objectives.

MARGINAL EFFECT IN HALTING VIOLENCE AGAINST KOSOVAR ALBANIANS

NATO Secretary General Solana, President Clinton, and various high U.S. officials declared a principal goal of NATO air operations to be deterring or halting violence against Kosovar Albanians. But Operation Allied Force had little direct effect on this violence. At the beginning of the operation, NATO was prepared to conduct only a few days of attacks against a limited set of targets. It had not deployed forces nor evolved procedures to conduct an effective effort against Yugoslav fielded military units in Kosovo. The result was a major gap between stated ends and then-available means. Yugoslav forces conducted large-scale ethnic cleansing during April with little impediment from NATO. As time went on, NATO deployed more aircraft that were well suited to the ground attack role, including U.S. A-10s and U.K. Harriers. NATO improved surveillance against Yugoslav forces using Predator unmanned aerial vehicles and human intelligence, while streamlining procedures to exploit this intelligence. In addition, TF Hawk contributed targeting data derived from Hunter unmanned aerial vehicles (UAVs), Q-37 radar, and human intelligence. As a result, NATO air attacks against deployed Serb forces in Kosovo became somewhat more effective, but Yugoslav forces still controlled Kosovo and continued their attacks on the KLA and civilian population there. Figure 3.3 shows the flow of refugees during the first several weeks of Operation Allied Force.

Several assessments of the effects of the air campaign against the fielded Yugoslav military in Kosovo were made: some immediately after the bombing stopped, others completed after extensive analysis of bomb damage assessment data and on-site inspections. In addition, corroborating evidence of damage was available from international inspection regimes. The message is mixed, but the available evidence overwhelmingly indicates that the damage was relatively modest.

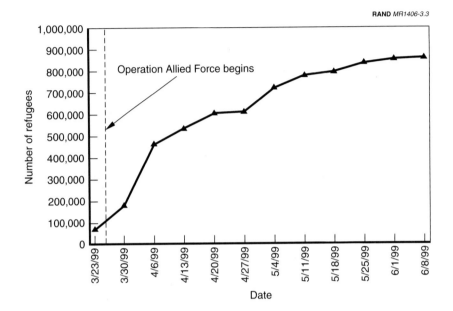

RAND *MR1406-3.3*

SOURCE: Report of the Organization for Security and Cooperation in Europe Kosovo Verification Mission.

Figure 3.3—Refugee Flow, March 23 to June 8, 1999

Joint Chiefs of Staff Briefing, June 10, 1999

At the end of Operation Allied Force, the U.S. Joint Chiefs of Staff presented a briefing summarizing NATO's effort.[48] That briefing depicted a doubling of non-U.S. strike aircraft (102 to 212) and a tripling of U.S. strike aircraft (112 to 323) during the operation. It showed that strike sorties peaked in late May at over 250 sorties/day as the force had grown and weather improved. As for outcomes, the briefing stated that Yugoslav military industry was "crippled," electrical power "down or unreliable," and fuel "limited." It maintained

---

[48]Joint Chiefs of Staff, "Operation Allied Force," Briefing, Unclassified, Washington, D.C., June 10, 1999.

that the Yugoslav army had suffered an "increasing number of APC, Artillery, and Tank losses."

The Joint Chiefs of Staff briefing showed relatively negligible Serb losses until May, small losses until late May, and dramatically escalating losses from May 29 through June 10. It gave approximate numbers of items affected by NATO strikes in three categories: tanks, armored personnel carriers (APCs), and artillery and mortars (see Table 3.1). The briefing did not specify whether these numbers related to destruction, damage, or engagement, but during the briefing Secretary of Defense Cohen and Major General (USAF) Charles F. Wald offered clarification. Secretary Cohen stated: "Most important, we severely crippled the military forces in Kosovo by destroying more than 50 percent of the artillery and more than one-third of the armored vehicles."[49] With reference to the slide, Wald stated: "So as you move across you can see that the numbers as we bring the air defense down, as the weather starts to get better, as the number of assets in the area increase, the numbers of kills of fielded forces starts to increase also."[50]

Table 3.1

Attacks on Fielded Forces

Source	Tanks and Self-Propelled Artillery	Armored Personnel Carriers	Artillery and Mortars
Dept of Defense/Joint Staff	120	220	450
SHAPE	93	153	389
Newsweek Magazine	14	18	20

SOURCES: Secretary of Defense William Cohen and Chairman of the Joint Chiefs of Staff Hugh Shelton, "Operation Allied Force," Briefing, Pentagon, Washington, D.C., June 10, 1999; General Wesley Clark, Supreme Allied Commander Europe, and Brigadier General (USAF) John Corley, Chief, Kosovo Mission Effectiveness Assessment Team, NATO headquarters, Mons, Belgium, September 11, 1999; John Barry and Evan Thomas, "The Kosovo Cover-Up," *Newsweek*, May 15, 2000, pp. 23–26; John Barry, "Newsweek and the 14 Tanks," *Air Force Magazine*, August 2000, pp. 6–7.

---

[49]William S. Cohen, General (USA) Henry H. Shelton, Major General (USAF) Charles F. "Chuck" Wald, Department of Defense News Briefing, Unclassified, Pentagon, Washington, D.C., 4:05 P.M., June 10, 1999.

[50]Ibid.

NATO SHAPE Briefing, September 16, 1999

On September 16, General Clark and Brigadier General John D. W. Corley provided a more detailed Kosovo strike assessment. Clark said that air strikes "forced the Yugoslav military and police heavy equipment into hiding; that these forces were unable to conduct their planned, unrestricted operations against the Albanian population in Kosovo or against the Kosovo Liberation Army . . ." He added that "the results are not so far off what we believed them to be at the end of the war."[51] "There were over 3,000 missions flown over Kosovo. In almost 2,000 of them pilots dropped weapons, they believed, on something, and we have assessed those claims and looked at it."[52] In response to a question from the *Washington Post*, Clark said: "A lot of it was taken out, just as we anticipated, because we never thought that we'd destroyed the whole of it. We never thought we'd destroyed even half of what was there. What we had been successful in doing was keeping it in hiding, under wraps, ineffective."[53]

Corley stated that his team had evaluated almost 2,000 pilot reports concerning mobile targets in Kosovo and validated more than half as "successful strikes." A "successful strike" implied that a strike aircraft delivered ordnance on what appeared to be a valid target, as confirmed by at least two sources from the following list: aircraft mission reports, on-site findings, interviews with forward air controllers, cockpit video, comparison of prestrike imagery with poststrike imagery, and human intelligence. Assessors visited 429 different locations specified in mission reports. They found relatively few pieces of catastrophically destroyed equipment, for example 26 in the tank category, but "We found extensive evidence of the Yugoslavs quickly removing damaged equipment from the battlefield."[54] Moreover, air crews repeatedly said that "equipment struck the previous day was no longer in the same location . . . ."[55]

---

[51]General Wesley K. Clark and Brigadier General John Corley, Press Conference on the Kosovo Strike Assessment, Headquarters, Supreme Allied Command Europe, Mons, Belgium, September 16, 1999.

[52]Ibid.

[53]Ibid.

[54]Ibid.

[55]Ibid.

Corley concluded that "successful strikes" were somewhat lower than the numbers given earlier by the Joint Chiefs of Staff (see again Table 3.1). By applying its methodology, the team found that in one-third to one-half of all cases there was insufficient evidence to validate a "successful strike," i.e., there was no additional corroborating source. The team also discovered examples of multiple strikes on the same targets and some strikes on decoys.

During the briefing, a Reuters representative asked General Clark whether a B-52 strike had destroyed large formations of Yugoslav forces in the Mount Pastrik region, as part of what was called "Operation Arrow." Clark replied that area bombing did not generate video as precision-guided weapons would and asked a pilot to give his description. The pilot said, "Quite a few vehicles were destroyed in a particular area."[56]

The Allied Force Munitions Effectiveness Assessment Team

The Allied Force Munitions Effectiveness Assessment Team was commissioned by General Clark to study weapons effects. This team had thirty military members with appropriate specialties, including operations, intelligence, targeting, and ordnance disposal. Team membership was predominantly American, but it included three French officers and one Italian officer. It visited almost all sites identified in mission reports but found few pieces of destroyed equipment. Almost all of the destroyed equipment was on the shoulders of roads or near roads. The team found no drag marks to indicate that damaged equipment had been removed. Despite extensive ground reconnaissance, the team found no destroyed equipment or fragments of equipment in the Mount Pastrik area. John Barry, a *Newsweek* national security correspondent, received data from the Allied Force Munitions Effectiveness Assessment Team report and published it in an article intended to refute what Barry considered to be inflated estimates of effectiveness.[57] These numbers are also shown in Table 3.1.

---

[56]Ibid.

[57]John Barry and Evan Thomas, "The Kosovo Cover-Up," *Newsweek*, May 15, 2000, pp. 23–26.

Annual Data Exchange, Sub-Regional Arms Control

Under the Agreement on Sub-Regional Arms Control signed in Florence, Italy, on June 14, 1996, the Federal Republic of Yugoslavia accepted numerical limits on its holdings of tanks, armored combat vehicles, artillery, combat aircraft, and attack helicopters. Parties to this agreement have the right to conduct inspections under escort by the inspected party. They exchange data annually in formats specified by protocol. Aside from concerns over the basic veracity of Yugoslavia's post-Kosovo submission, data submitted cannot substitute for battle damage assessment because many causes other than combat might account for inventory changes. However, annual data exchanges are one indicator of trends in overall Yugoslav equipment holdings. They suggest that these holdings declined only slightly during the year in which Operation Allied Force was conducted, as depicted in Table 3.2.

Summary of Strike Assessments

The extent of damage to Yugoslav equipment in Kosovo remains uncertain, but it seems unlikely that many systems were catastrophically destroyed. What happened in those strikes where no hulks were found? Given targeting uncertainties and inherent inaccuracies of even the precision-guided weapons, some strikes may have missed by enough distance to leave hard targets undamaged, especially tanks. Other strikes may have caused minor damage, such as a damaged track, and still others may have caused major damage, such as loss of an engine, that could be repaired on site.

The Allied Force Munitions Effectiveness Assessment Team may have missed some hulks, but probably not many because it tried to inspect all sites identified in mission reports. Yugoslav forces might have removed some hulks, but again probably not many because it had few heavy equipment movers and was constantly exposed to air attack. Moreover, it is unclear why Yugoslav forces would have run the risk to remove unserviceable equipment. No count was made of equipment crossing from Kosovo into Yugoslavia proper after the conflict, but departing Yugoslav units appeared combat effective with high morale and displaying large holdings of undamaged equipment. This generally good appearance suggests that Yugoslav forces suffered little damage beyond the hulks left in place in Kosovo.

Table 3.2

Yugoslav Annual Data Exchanges

Equipment Type or Category	1999	2000	Change
T-55 main battle tank	721	721	None
T-72 main battle tank	65	65	None
M-84 main battle tank (T-72 copy)	239	230	−9
Total for main battle tanks	**1,025**	**1,016**	**−9**
BOV VP M-86 armored personnel carrier	69	58	−11
OT M-60 armored personnel carrier	150	147	−3
BVP M-80 infantry combat vehicle	568	562	−6
Total for APC/IFV	**787**	**767**	**−20**
H 105mm M-56 (Yugoslav-built)	265	260	−5
H 122mm D-30	310	303	−7
H 122mm M-38	90	89	−1
H 155mm M-1	139	137	2
H 155mm M-65	6	6	None
T 130mm M-46	276	256	−20
TH 152mm D-20	25	25	None
TH 152mm NORA (Yugoslav-built ~D-20)	52	52	None
SH 122mm 2S1 Gvozdika (self-propelled)	83	82	−1
Total for artillery	**1,246**	**1,210**	**−36**
MB 82mm M-69	1,086	1,103	+17
MB 120mm M-74	283	283	None
MB 120mm M-75	798	802	+4
Total for mortars	**2,167**	**2,188**	**+21**
Total for artillery and mortars	**3,413**	**3,398**	**−15**

NOTE: Numerical equipment designators are specified in the Agreement on Sub-Regional Arms Control, Appendix 1, "List of Notification Formats."

SOURCES: Federal Republic of Yugoslavia, Agreement on Sub-Regional Arms Control, Information on the Army of Yugoslavia, Annual Data Exchange, Valid as of January 01, 1999, unclassified; Federal Republic of Yugoslavia, Information on Armaments Limited by the Agreement on Sub-Regional Arms Control in Federal Republic of Yugoslavia, Entry into Force January 01, 2000, unclassified.

By not presenting Serb forces with a credible opposing ground threat and by not making full use of all available targeting assets against the fielded forces, air-land synergies went largely unrealized. The limits of the KLA as an opposing ground force, even with NATO air support, were best exemplified in Operation Arrow. The aim of this effort was to link with other KLA forces operating in the interior of Kosovo. In the course of this operation, the KLA heavily engaged Yugoslav forces in the area of Mount Pastrik near Goruzup. Despite NATO air attacks, including B-52 strikes, the KLA suffered heavily from Yugoslav counterattacks and was repulsed nearly to its starting positions. Admiral Ellis thought that "Air strikes were effective against Yugoslav armor only after the KLA launched its major offensive."[58] But a search of the Mount Pastrik area later revealed no destroyed equipment.

Finally, despite NATO command of the air, the number of Yugoslav ground forces in Kosovo more than tripled during the fighting. Likewise, the successful damage inflicted on the Yugoslav army infrastructure and logistics was mitigated by the fact that Serb forces did not have to conduct high-tempo operations against a serious land adversary. Another key synergy therefore went unexploited.

---

[58]Admiral James O. Ellis, (USN), "A View from the Top," unpublished briefing, Naples, Italy: Headquarters, U.S. Naval Forces, Europe, undated.

Chapter Four

TASK FORCE HAWK

Task Force Hawk was intended to provide an additional means for hitting Milosevic's fielded forces with a deep-strike capability using AH-64 Apache attack helicopters and the Multiple Launch Rocket System (MLRS). But the concept of operations for TF Hawk raised difficult questions. How could a relatively small number of Apaches make an appreciable difference at acceptable risk to themselves? How could the MLRS, an element in suppressing Serb air defenses as part of deep-strike operations, be employed without risking collateral damage that would discredit NATO? Most senior military leadership in Washington was skeptical about the concept and opposed deployment of TF Hawk. When the theater commander continued to advocate deployment, the issue was resolved at higher levels in favor of General Clark. But when two Apache pilots were killed in training accidents in Albania, whatever inclination there was to employ the task force quickly dissipated. As will be recounted in this chapter, however, TF Hawk did contribute to the ultimate success of Operation Allied Force, but in ways that were not readily apparent to outside observers. It also met its designated deployment schedule under demanding conditions. But seen from outside, TF Hawk was widely regarded as slow, cumbersome, and a failure that hurt the Army's reputation. A detailed look at the operation reveals a more complex story.

ORIGIN AND CONTROVERSY

The concept for TF Hawk emerged from a conversation in mid-March 1999 between General Clark and General Shelton, Chairman of the U.S. Joint Chiefs of Staff.[1] Following this conversation, Clark considered using an Army attack helicopter strike force as part of the NATO air operation. On March 20, General Clark and Admiral Ellis were at Grafenwöehr, Germany, to observe a Battle Command Training Program "Warfighter" exercise by the 1st Armored Division. Elements of V Corps Headquarters, the 11th Aviation Regiment, and V Corps Artillery also participated.[2] Much of the Battle Command Training Program was devoted to deep-attack operations by Army aviation units. During this exercise, Clark and Ellis discussed the feasibility of using attack helicopters to complement NATO fixed-wing air operations, now only days away. The meeting concluded with a decision to request deployment of Army helicopters. That same day, U.S. Army Europe and V Corps received their first warning of the prospective mission. These headquarters started planning immediately, but Operation Allied Force was now only four days off.[3] This was in marked contrast to the lengthy planning times available to prepare for fixed-wing air operations.

V Corps' mission was to provide a deep-attack capability in northern Macedonia based on attack helicopters and the MLRS armed with rockets and the Army Tactical Missile System (ATACMS). In the CINC's judgment, the attack helicopters and rocket launchers would provide an additional capability with which to strike the Yugoslav ground forces in Kosovo; a capability different from that provided by high-flying fixed-wing aircraft. Corps planners intended to build the TF Hawk organization based on the mission, but they were con-strained by force caps mandated by higher headquarters.[4] The initial cap was approximately 2,000 and, in early April, approximately 2,500 troops. By March 22, V Corps planners had developed an initial concept for the employment of TF Hawk, but they did so in the

---

[1]RAND interviews, November 5, 1999.

[2]Draft, "Operation Victory Hawk After Action Report," U.S. Army Europe Lessons Learned Office, November 3, 1999.

[3]General Clark notes that just prior to the launching of Operation Allied Force he was told that General Shelton was very keen to get the Apaches into the operation if General Clark wanted them. Clark, *Waging Modern War*, p. 181.

[4]"Operation Victory Hawk After Action Report"; interviews at V Corps conducted in Heidelberg, Germany, November 10, 1999.

absence of an overall NATO campaign plan to guide the use of Army deep-attack capabilities.[5]

While Army planners in Europe worked to refine their initial task organization and deployment plan, Clark submitted a request to the Joint Chiefs of Staff for an Army attack helicopter strike force. Simultaneously, V Corps and U.S. Army Europe received a formal warning order to be prepared to form and deploy a helicopter task force to Macedonia. The U.S. European Command warning order specified that deployment might be required within the next seven days.

The Decision to Deploy Task Force Hawk

The decision to deploy TF Hawk was controversial. From mid-March through the presidential decision to deploy TF Hawk on April 3, opinions differed sharply over the advisability of deploying Apaches. General Clark intended TF Hawk to be integrated into NATO's air operations, initially as an element of the U.S.-only Joint Task Force Noble Anvil. It was to be a deep-attack force, attacking dispersed Yugoslav forces. In addition to growing political pressure to hit fielded forces in Kosovo, General Clark believed destroying even relatively small numbers of these ground forces could have significant effects on Belgrade's determination to continue the war.

When the Joint Staff in Washington received General Clark's request for TF Hawk on March 26, the proposal was staffed among the four services, two days after air operations had begun. The initial concept reviewed by the services and the Joint Staff assumed that TF Hawk would deploy to Macedonia, not Albania. Even under that more favorable assumption, the services raised concerns. After the switch to Albania on March 29, the Army, Air Force, and Marine Corps nonconcurred on Clark's request. Among the reasons cited by the Army:

- Deployment of TF Hawk would introduce ground forces, contrary to U.S. policy.

- There were few lucrative targets given the dispersed nature of Yugoslav forces.

---

[5]Unpublished V Corps Task Force Hawk briefing, March 22, 1999.

- Yugoslav forces would pose a significant threat to the force.

- The task force was too unconventional in employing attack helicopters without a maneuver ground force.[6]

The Navy had major concerns about a proposal to fire the ATACMS from its ships, an idea that appeared in the initial concept from General Clark. The Air Force was concerned about the burden placed on its airlift in deploying TF Hawk. Marine Corps objections focused on the potential vulnerability of the Apaches and potentially high loss rates.

Given nonconcurrence by the Army, Air Force, and Marine Corps, the prospects for deployment of TF Hawk appeared slim. On April 1, a videoteleconference was held in which General Clark and Lieutenant General Hendrix, Commander V Corps, briefed the Secretary of Defense, the Chairman of the Joint Chiefs of Staff, and the Service Chiefs on the proposed Apache mission. Many questions were raised about the proposed operation by the Pentagon officials, and the meeting ended without a decision.[7] But on April 2, a Joint Staff action was circulated to all services with a draft message authorizing deployment of TF Hawk to Albania.[8] While noting that final approval for the task force by the National Command Authorities was still pending, the draft message indicated a shift in deployment prospects. Apparently deliberations were in progress concerning TF Hawk, with the National Security Council aware of the intense debate going on within the Defense Department regarding the advisability of deploying the unit. Reportedly, the National Security Council regarded TF Hawk as an operational issue that the Department of Defense should resolve.[9]

The Secretary of Defense and the Chairman of the Joint Chiefs of Staff finally recommended to the National Security Council that TF Hawk be deployed based on General Clark's request. This recom-

---

[6]Dana Priest, "Risks and Restraint: Why the Apaches Never Flew in Kosovo," *The Washington Post,* December 29, 1999, p. A1.

[7]Clark, *Waging Modern War,* pp. 230–232.

[8]Unpublished Joint Action draft message, April 2, 1999.

[9]RAND interview, January 2000.

mendation persuaded the National Security Council to recommend deployment to the President.[10]

On April 3, formal authorization was granted for the deployment of TF Hawk to Albania, and a Joint Chiefs of Staff deployment order was issued on April 4. Whether TF Hawk would also be employed in combat remained to be determined. The presidential decision to deploy TF Hawk was clearly separate from a decision to actually employ the Apaches. The controversy over employment continued among senior military leaders; it remained unresolved as the war ended in June. But at the time of the deployment, Army planners in Europe had to assume that the force would be used.[11]

The Change to Albania

While negotiations continued with the Macedonian government in late March and the Joint Staff in Washington debated whether to deploy TF Hawk, Army planners in Europe fleshed out the organizational and deployment details of the force. As originally envisioned, TF Hawk was to be built around elements of two AH-64A Apache battalions. U.S. Army Europe assumed that eventually 48 Apaches (2 full battalions) would deploy, but the initial planning was based on 24 aircraft, in accordance with guidance from General Clark. Additionally, several batteries of MLRS would be included in the task force to provide deep fires into Kosovo, especially to suppress enemy air defenses. The original composition of TF Hawk is shown in Figure 4.1. The force comprised some 1,700 Soldiers, 24 Apaches, and 22 support helicopters.[12] At this stage, Army planners in Europe assumed that the force would deploy to Macedonia, where substantial NATO force protection and support elements were already present (primarily elements of the Allied Command Europe Rapid Reac-

---

[10]Secretary of Defense William Cohen, interview with *Frontline*, PBS, and RAND interviews with other participants, April 12, 2000.

[11]This episode also led to controversy over the relative roles of the combatant commanders, the Chairman, the Joint Chiefs, and the services in making and advising on decisions for forces, raising issues of interpretation and intent of the Goldwater-Nichols legislation.

[12]V Corps Task Force Hawk briefing; "Operation Victory Hawk After Action Report."

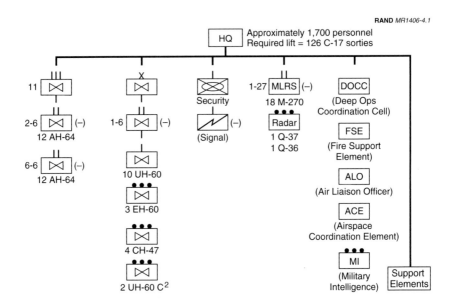

Figure 4.1—Initial Task Force Hawk Structure (Macedonia)

tion Corps). Consequently, only one infantry company was included to provide security.

The initial composition of TF Hawk reflects the deep-attack emphasis of the unit's mission. Elements of two Apache attack helicopter battalions were the centerpiece of the organization. Complementing the attack helicopters were two batteries of MLRS rocket launchers (9 launchers per battery) and several Firefinder artillery- and mortar-locating radars. The MLRS were intended to suppress VJ air defense sites to facilitate strikes by the Apaches. The Firefinder radars would be able to pinpoint VJ and MUP artillery and mortar units firing against the KLA in western Kosovo.

Various support helicopters were also part of the task force. These included UH-60 Blackhawks and CH-47 Chinooks for medical evacuation as well as transport of fuel, ammunition, and other supplies. Additionally, several EH-60s were included for electronic warfare missions.

The fact that the initial planning assumed the task force would deploy to Macedonia is reflected in its organization. As previously stated, only one infantry company was included for protection of the task force's base areas. With a large NATO force already in Macedonia, the planners at V Corps obviously felt that minimal numbers of additional ground combat units would be required to protect the force.

Command and control and support elements rounded out the 1,700-person initial organization. Given the deep-attack mission, portions of the Corps Force Support Element, Airspace Coordination Element, and Deep Attack Coordination Cell were in the organization. In addition, the Corps Air Liaison Officer from the Air Force was also part of the task force.

On March 29, the Macedonian government announced its decision to prohibit offensive operations from its soil.[13] That same day, a V Corps reconnaissance party flew to Italy and Albania to begin the process of exploring the possibility of deploying to Albania should Macedonia continue to refuse to permit offensive operations, and hence deployment of TF Hawk on its territory. This initial reconnaissance party returned on March 31. Despite a March 30 appeal from NATO Secretary General Solana to the government of Macedonia, it still refused approval.[14] This refusal eliminated the preferred basing option for the task force. On April 2, U.S. Army Europe and V Corps were informed that TF Hawk probably would not be approved. But meanwhile, negotiations with the government of Albania to accept the task force were nearing completion.[15]

---

[13]"Operation Victory Hawk After Action Report."

[14]Interviews with U.S. European Command, November 12, 1999.

[15]At this same time planning for another U.S. Army deployment, Task Force Thunder, was under way and itself running into political problems. One week after the start of Operation Allied Force, the Supreme Headquarters Allied Powers Europe requested the deployment of a task force built around batteries of the MLRS using ATACMS. Separate from Task Force Hawk, the mission of this task force was to be suppression of Yugoslav air defenses throughout Yugoslavia. Originally planned for Croatia to provide the range necessary to hit air defense sites in the northern portion of Yugoslavia, this option was opposed by the State Department on political grounds relating to the 1995 Dayton accords. Hungary was then approached, but it had its own political problems with the idea of missiles launched from its soil. The task force was never deployed.

Humanitarian operations to aid the refugees pouring out of Kosovo were already under way in Albania (NATO Operation Allied Harbour and U.S. Operation Shining Hope). On April 1, the Albanian government agreed to NATO's requests to base a humanitarian force in their country. That same day, General Clark directed that if TF Hawk were approved, it would deploy to Albania. On April 3, V Corps planners learned that President Clinton had approved the mission. They immediately dispatched a small reconnaissance team to Albania to assess infrastructure and determine exactly where TF Hawk should deploy. On April 4, the Joint Chiefs of Staff issued an Execute Order, and another V Corps reconnaissance team departed for Albania on April 5.[16]

Although Allied Forces Southern Europe had conducted an engineering study of Albania roughly two years earlier,[17] V Corps planners had relatively little information immediately available on Europe's poorest nation. The Deputy V Corps Commander, Major General (USA) Julian Burns, led the team that went to Albania on April 5. There was a need to determine quickly where TF Hawk should deploy. Options were limited to Gjader airfield in the northern part of Albania, and Rinas airport outside Tiranë. Apparently, the potential for deploying part of the force by sea into the relatively shallow port of Durrës was not considered at this time.

V Corps had to balance speed of deployment with the degree of risk to which the force would be exposed. Gjader airfield was quickly ruled out by Lieutenant General John W. Hendrix, the V Corps Commander, and Colonel Raymond T. Odierno[18] because Gjader was within range of long-range Yugoslav artillery in Montenegro. The planners therefore selected Rinas airport, where humanitarian operations were already in progress. The reconnaissance of Rinas, conducted by V Corps operations planners, logistics staff officers, and an Air Force air mobility representative, showed that there was limited

---

[16]Interviews with U.S. European Command, November 12, 1999; "Operation Victory Hawk After Action Report."

[17]Interview with V Corps planners, conducted in Heidelberg, Germany, on November, 10, 1999. Several days into the planning, V Corps obtained a copy of the extant AFSOUTH study of Albania.

[18]Now Major General (USA) Raymond T. Odierno, originally designated as Task Force Hawk commander.

runway and ramp space (see Figure 4.2). The area off the runway became unusable due to extremely heavy rain, forcing a relocation of the helicopter parking area as well as the construction of individual pads for the aircraft.

The reconnaissance team assessed that TF Hawk could be deployed by April 23, the target date established by General Clark, while the airport continued to support humanitarian flights. The team calculated that a maximum of three C-17 aircraft dedicated to TF Hawk could be on the ground at the same time (maximum on ground or MOG). The original timelines assumed day-only visual flight rules, and they were based on the original size of the force, roughly 1,700 personnel. But during this reconnaissance, weather was good and

RAND *MR1406-4.2*

SOURCE: U.S. Department of Defense.

Figure 4.2—Rinas Airport at Tiranë

the ground was dry at Rinas.[19] Persistent rains would later generate muddy conditions that severely hampered movement off the tarmac and hardstand.

The deployment of TF Hawk was publicly announced during a Department of Defense press briefing on April 4. Mr. Kenneth H. Bacon, the Assistant Secretary of Defense, Public Affairs, responding to a question about how quickly the MLRS and Apaches could move to Albania, stated that "You're probably talking, when you consider the transportation challenges, probably talking about a week or so, maybe seven to ten days, I would guess . . . ." A formal Department of Defense press release that same day stated that it "will take up to ten days to deploy the units."[20] This statement implied closure on April 14, well before Clark's target date.[21]

Deployment of Task Force Hawk

This operation approximated a "no notice" deployment. Even though planning staffs in Europe had about seven days notice that they would be deploying to Albania instead of Macedonia, they were prevented from accomplishing required preparations for fear of violating the Roberts Amendment. The Roberts Amendment barred the Department of Defense from spending appropriated funds to deploy U.S. forces to Macedonia, Albania, or Yugoslavia until the President certified the need to Congress.[22] As a result, Army logistics planners

---

[19]Interviews with Task Force Hawk participants, December 3, 1999.

[20]DoD Defense Link, DoD News Briefing, April 4, 1999, and *U.S. Attack Helicopters and Multiple Launch Rocket Systems to Deploy in Support of Operation Allied Force*, DoD Press Release No. 145-99, April 4, 1999; *DoD News Briefing*, April 4, 1999, Mr. Kenneth H. Bacon, Assistant Secretary of Defense for Public Affairs.

[21]Where the "seven to ten days" figure originated was never adequately resolved in our research. General Clark himself reports in his account that "We had a number of Apache crews and controllers based in Germany, and we estimated that once we were given the go-ahead it might take a week or ten days to get them into the theater of operations." Clark, *Waging Modern War,* p. 198. But this statement refers to his estimate when the task force was still slated for Macedonia and to consist of about 1,700 troops. It is possible that this original estimate was used by the Pentagon Office of Public Affairs despite the substantial change in conditions and associated timelines with the later shift to Albania.

[22]The Roberts Amendment was attached to the FY 1999 Department of Defense Appropriations Act as Section 8115.

could not enter Albania in advance of the force to assess available infrastructure, plan operations, acquire real estate, preposition reception equipment, or improve existing facilities to receive, stage, and move the force. The Army had an existing contract with the firm of Brown and Root to support operations in the Balkans. Brown and Root could have sent management personnel and support equipment immediately to Albania with a "notice to proceed," acquired local national workers and other resources, and improved some basic reception and staging facilities before the arrival of the combat force, but this was not pursued because it was viewed as a potential violation of the amendment. The Defense Logistics Agency was not even able to prepurchase lumber or other necessary items specifically intended for improving the reception and staging activities. Relief from these restrictions came when the Roberts Amendment provisions were met by the Administration on April 4.

The deployment and sustainment of any large ground or air military units typically require coordinated use of both air and surface modes of transportation. Deployment planning often requires a balanced use of both modes to meet requirements. Albania presented a situation in which both air and surface modes were highly restricted.

Durrës, the main port serving Albania, is located approximately 50 kilometers from the airfield at Rinas, near the capital city Tiranë. It is a shallow-draft port with a small throughput capacity. The primary road linking Durrës and Tiranë is two lanes and of limited trafficability for heavy vehicles. Banditry in the local area posed a security problem. All bulk petroleum, oil, and lubricants, some deploying unit equipment, and much of the sustainment stocks had to use this road.

For its part, the airfield at Rinas had limited ability to handle a substantial volume of traffic. In February 1999, the airport handled fewer than ten flights per day. It lacked modern lighting systems and navigation and landing aids, and it operated only during daylight. As the Kosovo refugee crisis grew, Rinas airport became host to a number of organizations associated with humanitarian relief. It became the entry port and staging area for relief materiel from both governmental and nongovernmental organizations. Excluding the U.S. Army, at least 12 other organizations were flying helicopters out of Rinas. They included the United Nations High Commissioner for

Refugees, the International Red Cross, the World Food Program, and military detachments from the United Kingdom, France, Switzerland, Austria, Germany, the United Arab Emirates, Italy, Greece, and Spain. Rinas airport was capable of handling this volume during daylight operations only; however, most of the "good real estate" (i.e., hardstand or high ground) was already occupied before April 4, 1999, forcing the Army to negotiate for space around the airport. The competition for airfield space and airflow into Rinas between TF Hawk and other ongoing, non-U.S. operations continued throughout the deployment.

The decision to put TF Hawk into Rinas in Albania rather than Skopje in Macedonia affected airfield operations and task force deployment in a number of ways. First, deploying TF Hawk with any speed necessitated 24-hour operations at the airfield. Second, the volume of troops, aircraft, and other equipment more than absorbed all available improved space. Third, the combination of humanitarian airlift (i.e., the decision having been made to not interrupt humanitarian aid), normal commercial traffic, humanitarian helicopter operations, and C-17/C-130 TF Hawk deployment lift and the accompanying need to clear the reception area of cargo (and explosives) stretched the airfield's capacity. Poor weather compounded these issues. The airport normally receives an average of 3.2 inches of rain in April; however, it rained most days for the first month of the TF Hawk deployment, creating serious flooding and mud problems. The helicopter parking area identified during the initial site reconnaissance became a sea of mud following these rains, prompting the Deputy Commander for Aviation, Brigadier General Richard Cody, to delay the arrival of Apaches from Italy until April 21.[23] These environmental conditions also restricted clearance routes from the cargo ramp and thus slowed movement.

As it turned out, Rinas airport could accept only two C-17s and a small number of C-130 aircraft simultaneously. NATO controlled Balkan airspace, and all aircraft had to obtain a "slot time" to land at Rinas. The C-17s were scheduled in flights of two by the Regional Air

---

[23]Then–Brigadier General Richard Cody was brought in to be Deputy Commanding General for Aviation Operations for TF Hawk. With extensive experience in Army aviation, including Special Forces, he was at the time Assistant Division Commander, 4th Infantry Division (Mechanized), Fort Hood, Texas.

RAND *MR1406-4.3*

SOURCE: Defense Visual Information Center *(www.dodmedia.osd.mil)*.

Figure 4.3—Battling MOG and Mud: The Two C-17 Maximum at Rinas

Movement Control Center, which was part of the Combined Air Operation Center at Vicenza. The C-17s were paired due to ramp constraints at Rinas. Despite these problems, C-17 missions grew from fewer than 10 in the initial days to approximately 20 per day as the airfield was opened to 24-hour operations (as of April 12) and the process smoothed out.

The throughput capability of Rinas airport, while it continued to accommodate humanitarian flights, was the dominant constraint on the deployment of TF Hawk. Two C-17s were allowed on the ground at any one time, but this maximum on ground (MOG) was only one factor in a calculation that included airspace management, ramp availability, and time to unload the aircraft.

RAND *MR1406-4.4*

SOURCE: Photo courtesy of Dr. Bernard Rostker, Under Secretary of the Army.

Figure 4.4—Ground Conditions at Rinas, Early May

On April 8, the first transport aircraft carrying TF Hawk assets departed from Ramstein Air Force Base.[24] To bring TF Hawk's assets to bear as rapidly as possible, the bulk of cargo was consigned to be deployed by air, and most of that by C-17. C-17 airlifters were used regardless of whether the unit's point of origin was in the European theater or the United States, or whether the unit originated at or transited Ramstein.

The deployment of rotary-wing aircraft presented a special challenge. These aircraft included 24 AH-64 Apache attack helicopters, 23 UH-60 Black Hawk utility helicopters, and eight CH-47 Chinook cargo helicopters. All these aircraft self-deployed from Germany with stops at Camp Darby near Livorno, Pisa, and Brindisi in Italy. On April 14, TF Hawk helicopters began a phased self-deployment from Germany.[25] By April 18, all helicopters had arrived in Pisa, Italy, but they remained there for several days due to the lack of hardstand

---

[24]Unpublished Task Force Noble Anvil situation report, April 8, 1999.

[25]Unpublished Task Force Noble Anvil situation report, April 14, 1999.

at the Rinas airport, poor weather, and Italian concern over their ordnance load. At Rinas, humanitarian aid helicopters had sunk up to their fuselages in mud. To avoid this fate, the Army helicopters stayed in Italy until parking pads were prepared for them.[26] Poor weather in Italy also delayed the deployment.

On April 21, the first eleven AH-64 helicopters arrived at the Rinas airport, along with four CH-47s and 16 UH-60s. On April 26, the last six AH-64s arrived. Figure 4.5 depicts the location of TF Hawk's helicopters from the time they started to deploy from Germany to the time all aircraft closed in Albania.

In contrast to earlier deployment experiences, communication problems were notably reduced. However, there was an initial lag in establishing high-volume logistics communications between the task force and supply providers in Europe and the United States. This was caused by the change in deployment from Macedonia to Albania. The Army Materiel Command created a flyaway communications package based on commercially available technology to provide early logistics connectivity for contingencies such as this. U.S. Army Europe had procured one flyaway communications package for its mission in Bosnia. That flyaway communications package was scheduled to move from Bosnia to Camp Able Sentry in Macedonia when Army planners believed that TF Hawk would deploy there. But when the TF Hawk deployment was switched to Albania, that flyaway communications package did not deploy with it. Rather, Army Materiel Command sent a different flyaway communications package from the United States to Rinas. Consequently, there were no dedicated high-volume data communications links for the logistics unitsduring the first two weeks of the deployment.[27] Logistics tactical communication assets and other commercial capabilities, such as cell phones, provided interim connectivity.

The earliest-deploying logistics units were told that the terrorist threat was high and that ground protection forces might have to fight

---

[26]Interviews with Task Force Hawk participants, October 20, 1999,

[27]Unpublished Army Materiel Command Logistics Support Element–Europe (LSE-E) Situation Report, April 1999.

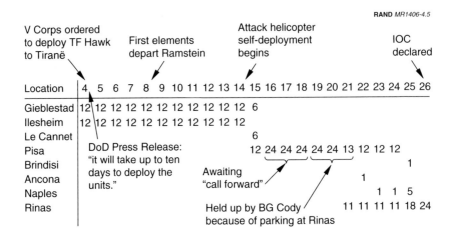

Figure 4.5—Task Force Hawk Helicopter Self-Deployment

within six hours of arrival.[28] Although this threat did not materialize, and Air Force personnel at Rinas supporting humanitarian operations were in soft caps and had light security, force protection continued to be the highest priority of TF Hawk during the first two weeks of operations in Albania. During that time, approximately 75 percent of the Army logistics personnel were consumed primarily with force protection—either installing perimeter defenses (primarily wire) or performing perimeter guard duties.

As early as April 8, the estimated size of TF Hawk had increased to roughly 3,660 personnel. Significant additions from the initial estimates included a mechanized infantry task force of battalion size, an air defense battery, engineers, a light infantry battalion, and additional logistics personnel.[29] The estimated size of the force continued to increase up to the point when the U.S. Army Europe Operations Plan was published on April 22.

---

[28]Interviews at 3d Support Command, U.S. V Corps, 7th Corps Support Group, Bamberg, Germany, November 9, 1999.

[29]Unpublished documents, U.S. Army Europe.

SOURCE: Defense Visual Information Center *(www.dodmedia.osd.mil).*

Figure 4.6—Army Apaches and Blackhawks Arriving at Rinas

Threat estimates were a major factor in determining TF Hawk's force
protection requirements. Army leaders and planners in Germany
had to account for the possibility that as soon as the task force
arrived in Albania, it could be at risk of Yugoslav attack, as well as
face challenges posed by the generally lawless situation in Albania.
Possible military threats to U.S. forces in Albania were estimated to
include Yugoslav aircraft raids, maneuver units of the Yugoslav 2nd
Army in Montenegro, Yugoslav commando and light infantry forces
crossing into Albania, and artillery and rocket fire from Montenegro
or Kosovo. Some intelligence estimates assessed that the Yugoslav
army could advance from Montenegro to Rinas in four hours and
advised V Corps and U.S. Army Europe accordingly. However, other
intelligence agencies assessed Yugoslav forces in Montenegro as
having little offensive capability. Clearly, the more conservative

estimates conducted in Europe drove the force protection provided for TF Hawk.

The resulting structure of TF Hawk is shown in Figure 4.7.

By the time the force was finalized in April, the size had more than tripled from the initial estimates made in late March. The force shown was composed of roughly 5,100 personnel. The major changes from the earliest versions of TF Hawk were due to increases in the organic force protection capabilities of the organization. Compared to a single mechanized infantry company in the original force, the final task force included a mechanized task force built around the 1-6 Infantry (Mechanized) with two companies of Bradley Fighting Vehicles and a company of Abrams main battle tanks. Additionally, the majority of a battalion of dismounted infantry from the 82nd Airborne Division, the 2-505th Parachute Infantry Regiment, had been added to the force. The indirect fires of the force had been supplemented by a third battery of MLRS (including a platoon capable of firing the extended-range Block 1A version of the

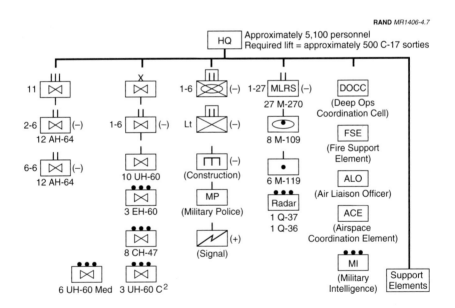

Figure 4.7—Task Force Hawk Structure

ATACMS), a battery of M-109A6 Paladin 155mm self-propelled how-itzers, and a battery of M-119 105mm towed howitzers. Due to the threat of fixed-wing aircraft from Montenegro, a battery of Avenger air defense systems was also added. Additional intelligence, military police, engineer, medical, and logistics personnel accounted for the remainder of the increase.[30] As summarized by General Clark,

> What had looked like an eight- to ten-day deployment of 1,800 troops to Macedonia, as I had originally envisaged and requested, was now bringing three times as many soldiers to Albania, into the middle of a more complex security environment at an overcrowded airport struggling to meet humanitarian requirements. That it was going to take only three times as long as originally estimated struck me as remarkable. I still hoped Hendrix would be able to make the first Apaches ready for a mission before the NATO summit on April 24. But the chances were diminishing with each day of weather delay.[31]

Despite the perception that TF Hawk was slow to deploy (aided by an unhelpful and inaccurate DoD press statement), it met required timelines. The National Security Council set a goal of April 24–25 for operational readiness of TF Hawk to coincide with the NATO 50-year summit held in Washington. The Supreme Allied Commander Europe then set the date at April 23. On that day, 11 attack heli-copters were at Rinas, with several mission readiness exercises already conducted. Furthermore, much of the support force for the task force had arrived. In all, deployment was a difficult task accomplished well by Army and Air Force personnel.

Still, in the final analysis many interrelated factors increased the time between the CINC's original request for TF Hawk on March 26 and the time at which it was reported as having full operational capability to conduct deep operations from Albania on May 7. These included:

- The late decision to consider attack helicopters as part of the phased air operation.

---

[30]Unpublished documents, U.S. Army Europe.

[31]Clark, *Waging Modern War,* p. 258.

- The need to plan for attack helicopter employment under unusual conditions in which there was no maneuver ground force.

- The early opposition from the Joint Chiefs of Staff to the CINC's request for the task force, in part due to skepticism over the concept of operations.

- The need to quickly adjust the composition and movement of the task force with the shift from Macedonia to Albania.

- The legislative restrictions on the predeployment advance site survey and reconnaissance parties.

- The competition for ramp space and airlift capacity at the limited Rinas airfield, compounded by confusing command arrangements and inclement weather.

- The initial need for ad hoc approaches for integrating TF Hawk into the ongoing air operation.

- The requirement for additional on-site training and rehearsals prior to combat operations to accommodate highly restrictive rules of engagement and to familiarize pilots with the unique terrain.

COMMAND AND CONTROL

The command and control arrangements for TF Hawk were complex, involving multiple chains of command. This was true both during its deployment and once it was operational in Albania. During deployment, General Montgomery Meigs, Commander, U.S. Army Europe, retained operational control of TF Hawk. After the deployment was completed, it was envisioned that General Clark, in his role as Supreme Allied Commander Europe, would assume NATO operational control and U.S. Army Europe would continue to control only certain residual functions. Supreme Allied Commander Europe would presumably pass NATO operational control to the Commander in Chief, Allied Forces Southern Europe, who might further delegate to a NATO land component commander if and when one was assigned. But TF Hawk actually remained under U.S. operational control when it was subordinated to Joint Task Force Noble Anvil on May 7.

Figure 4.8 shows the command relationship of TF Hawk to the other elements of Operation Allied Force. Although mentioned in the U.S. Army Europe Operations Plan, no land component commander was ever designated to coordinate the activities of U.S. and NATO ground forces in Albania and Macedonia. The TF Hawk commander, General Hendrix, became the senior U.S. Army commander conducting operations associated with Operation Allied Force. From this perspective, Hendrix stood at the same level as Lieutenant General Michael C. Short, the air component commander of AFSOUTH, who was also the senior U.S. Air Force commander.[32]

When the concept for TF Hawk was first discussed, it was planned that Colonel Odierno would assume command. When planning started, Colonel Odierno was serving as an Assistant Division Commander of the 1st Armored Division in Germany. As the size and complexity of the operation increased and as the relationship of TF

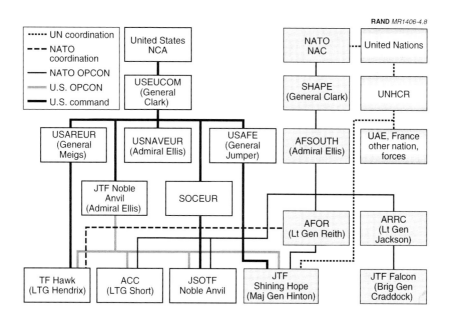

Figure 4.8—Task Force Hawk Command Relationships

---

[32]"Operation Victory Hawk After Action Report"; U.S. Army Europe documents.

Hawk to other U.S. and NATO elements became clearer, Hendrix assumed command of the task force. Once Hendrix deployed to Albania in early April, the Deputy V Corps Commander assumed responsibility for day-to-day operations of V Corps in Germany.[33]

Since TF Hawk's mission planning and concept of operation had to be integrated with the ongoing fixed-wing air operation, it was essential that its planning be integrated with the CAOC. The principal ways to integrate planning were through the air tasking order, the Joint Targeting Coordination Board located in Vicenza, and the Army Battlefield Coordination Element, co-located with the CAOC.

Command and Control at Rinas

U.S. doctrine emphasizes the importance of unity of command, but this did not exist at the Rinas airport. While the commander of U.S. Joint Task Force Shining Hope, Major General (USAF) William Hinton, Jr., believed that as the senior Air Force officer in Albania he had overall responsibility for the safe operation of Rinas airport, he had no authority over the commander of TF Hawk, General Hendrix, who was the senior U.S. military officer on the scene.

Joint Task Force Shining Hope handled the daily flow of humanitarian aid flights into the Rinas airport during daylight hours. These commercially chartered flights originated in the United States, Canada, Europe, the Near East, and Pakistan. They arrived in many different configurations, including some loads not on pallets. In addition, Joint Task Force Shining Hope controlled U.S. rotary-wing aircraft dedicated to humanitarian assistance from the USS *Inchon*. These helicopters flew sorties to and from the Kukës area near the Yugoslav border when the security situation permitted. Joint Task Force Shining Hope also helped coordinate all nonmilitary helicopters using Rinas airport for humanitarian purposes.[34] At the

---

[33]Interviews with Task Force Hawk participants, December 3, 1999, and with U.S. Army Europe Lessons Learned office, November 9, 1999.

[34]The French, in whose sector Rinas airport lay, initiated a system of call signs, check-in points, altitude assignment, flight procedures, and landing procedures for helicopters. The 86th Contingency Response Group (CRG) assured proper coordination with the Combined Air Operations Center in Vicenza and sponsored a helicopter working group, which met twice daily. Interviews with CRG personnel.

same time, U.S. Transportation Command lifted forces assigned to TF Hawk from Ramstein Air Force Base in Germany to Rinas airport by C-17.

As TF Hawk began to deploy to Rinas, operational differences and priorities emerged. General Hinton became concerned about flight safety. Vehicles assigned to TF Hawk drove on the runway, increasing the risk to jet engines of foreign object damage (largely dirt and mud). They reportedly approached aircraft before the engines shut down. In addition, TF Hawk stored ammunition near the side of the runway and had a road constructed too close to one end of the runway. In one alarming incident, an Army helicopter flew closer to an Air Force C-17 than was advisable by standard procedures. In a conversation on April 21, Hinton raised safety concerns with Hendrix, who agreed to comply with NATO safety standards. Coordination of rotary-wing flights improved quite rapidly, but the risk of foreign object damage was a less tractable problem. The taxiway often looked like a dirt road. Indeed, TF Hawk officers saw no alternative to crossing the runway until a bypass road was built. In addition, TF Hawk took weeks to relocate facilities, which were within the minimum distance of 150 meters from centerline prescribed by NATO standard.[35]

Due to their differing missions, the two commanders had widely differing perspectives. General Hinton thought that flight safety was a paramount concern, both for the humanitarian flights and for the C-17 flights supporting TF Hawk. General Hendrix and his immediate subordinates, General Cody, Deputy Commanding General for Aviation Operations, and Colonel Odierno, Deputy Commander for Fire Support and Ground Operations, were concerned that Yugoslav forces might attempt a surprise attack. They were focused on preparing for complex deep-attack operations as rapidly as possible under adverse conditions. This included crews practicing mission profiles for strikes into Kosovo under conditions of tight operational security.

Differing threat perceptions implied different standards of individual and organizational force protection as well. Joint Task Force Shining

---

[35]Interviews with Joint Task Force Shining Hope participants, December 29, 1999.

Hope personnel wore soft caps, while TF Hawk personnel wore body armor and helmets, although both were located in the same area. Joint Task Force Shining Hope felt sufficiently protected by elements of a Marine Corps infantry battalion around the perimeter. By contrast, TF Hawk deployed two Army infantry battalions (one mechanized and one light) to protect its operations at Rinas and at a forward operating base near the Kosovo border. More important, Joint Task Force Shining Hope operated the Rinas airport consistent with normal peacetime procedures, including radio contact between aircraft and tower. In contrast, TF Hawk had to operate in tactical fashion, observing radio silence. In particular, the AH-64 Apache attack helicopters practiced missions conducted in darkness without using radio communications, which Yugoslav forces might have intercepted.

TASK FORCE HAWK OPERATIONS

TF Hawk was formed to conduct deep-attack helicopter and missile strikes in conjunction with NATO's phased air operation. Although TF Hawk's helicopters and missiles were not employed, detailed planning and preparation took place in the event that they were ordered into combat. TF Hawk also contributed considerably to air operations by developing targets and providing intelligence to the CAOC in Vicenza.

Deep Operations Planning

Fielded forces in Kosovo proved to be elusive targets. Operating in small, dispersed units, the Yugoslav army took advantage of the cover and concealment provided by the small villages and heavy forestation in Kosovo. Sporadically poor weather also degraded the ability of NATO fighters operating at medium altitude to locate and strike Yugoslav forces operating in Kosovo and southern Yugoslavia. General Clark expected that TF Hawk's attack helicopters and missiles would be better suited to attack Yugoslav forces that were conducting ethnic cleansing and fighting the KLA inside Kosovo.

TF Hawk was operating in a somewhat unusual situation. Army deep-attack missions are normally conducted in conjunction with other ground force maneuver units.[36] This was not the case in Albania-Kosovo. Furthermore, no ground force area of operations had been allocated to TF Hawk by Allied Forces Southern Europe, nor had a land component commander been designated. As a consequence, there was some initial confusion over command relationships and procedures when it came to integrating Army attack helicopters into the air operation.[37]

Organizationally, General Hendrix, as TF Hawk's commander, like General Short, the AFSOUTH Air Component Commander, reported directly to Admiral Ellis, the Commander of Joint Task Force Noble Anvil. Nevertheless, TF Hawk's proposed missions had to be coordinated with NATO's air operations and the U.S.-only Noble Anvil missions.

To track the location of Yugoslav field forces, TF Hawk had access to multiple intelligence sources. These included national- and theater-level systems, organic systems, and unmanned aerial vehicles flown from Macedonia. National- and theater-level systems provided data primarily to the Joint Analysis Center in Molesworth, United Kingdom. Molesworth provided the U.S. European Command and TF Hawk with daily updates on Yugoslav forces.

Organic intelligence systems included the Q-37 Firefinder radar that was deployed to a forward operating base some 20 kilometers south of the Albania-Kosovo border. The Q-37 located numerous Yugoslav artillery and mortar units that were engaging the KLA. However, the mountainous terrain reduced the radar's effective range. The task force also had several UH-60 Quick Fix helicopters and RC-12 Guardrail electronic warfare aircraft to gather electronic intelligence on Yugoslav forces in Kosovo.

---

[36]Deep attack is a normal mission for Army attack helicopters. However, doctrine also stresses that deep attack must be coordinated with other elements of a combined arms team. See Field Manual 1-112, *Attack Helicopter Operations*, Department of the Army, 1997.

[37]Joint Pub 3-0, *Operations*, states that joint force commanders may define areas of operations for land and naval forces (p. II-19). During Operation Allied Force, no land component area of operations was established.

Mission Planning

TF Hawk's focal point for mission planning was the V Corps Deep Operations Coordination Cell, which deployed to Albania from Germany. In normal operations, the Deep Operations Coordination Cell would represent only a portion of a corps' planning effort, since deep operations normally complement the close operations of other maneuver forces. In this situation, however, deep operations were the main mission of TF Hawk. Therefore, the planning activities of the Deep Operations Coordination Cell were of paramount importance. TF Hawk's staff, including the Deep Operations Coordination Cell, had to be augmented by V Corps resources, thus reducing the capability of the staff that remained in Germany.

Based on the nature of the mission, the Deep Operations Coordination Cell was augmented with various capabilities to ensure that it could adequately plan operations. For example, initially the Deep Operations Coordination Cell did not have a targeting/planning cell. This function was assigned to the 11th Attack Helicopter Regiment's Tactical Operations Center, which was co-located with the Deep Operations Coordination Cell. Due to the restrictive rules of engagement, it was necessary to monitor the locations of civilian refugees and the KLA simultaneously with the ongoing targeting of Yugoslav forces. Therefore, the Deep Operations Coordination Cell established three cells that tracked locations of civilians, the KLA, and Yugoslav forces on a daily basis.[38]

Although originally deployed to Macedonia under Task Force Hunter, Army Hunter UAVs were eventually placed under the operational control of TF Hawk to assist in targeting. Hunter missions were planned three days in advance, with refinements taking place until the day a mission was flown. Mission taskings were sent to Task Force Hunter via a liaison officer located with TF Hawk.

Targeting was complicated and continuous. TF Hawk focused its targeting effort on Yugoslav army maneuver units operating in southwest Kosovo. Key Yugoslav army targets included armored

---

[38]Unpublished document from the Center for Army Lessons Learned, "Task Force Hawk in Operation Allied Force," Initial Impressions Report, September 1999; interview with Task Force Hawk participant, December 3, 1999.

vehicles, artillery, air defense systems, command and control nodes, and troop concentrations. The weapon systems and sensors of the AH-64 are optimized for the location and identification of these types of targets. By the time TF Hawk reported full operational capability, May 7, Yugoslav forces had been under NATO air attack for six weeks and had developed tactics to minimize their exposure. When not required to maneuver, infantry and armored vehicles would hide in forests and among buildings. Their artillery would fire against KLA targets, normally moving after a few fire missions. These tactics proved effective in minimizing the ability of NATO aircraft to locate small units operating in Kosovo. The targeting cell of TF Hawk relied heavily on Hunter unmanned aerial vehicles and the Q-37 counter-fire radars. Often, Hunters would be sent to locations identified by the radars to confirm the presence of Yugoslav army units in that area. Additionally, during May, reports from the KLA became an important source of intelligence and targeting information for TF Hawk. Data from these sources was collated by the Deep Operations Coordination Cell to develop a picture of Yugoslav forces operating in southwestern Kosovo.

The terrain along the Albania-Kosovo border limited the number of flight routes to seven passes through the mountains. Figure 4.9 illustrates a planned TF Hawk deep-attack mission. As shown in the diagram, attack helicopters would have been part of a coordinated package that included fires against Yugoslav air defense, interaction with the EC-130E/J Airborne Command and Control Center, supporting AC-130 gunships, and helicopters to conduct search and rescue. Army aircraft would have flown in small groups along pre-selected routes to designated areas where short, violent engagements against Yugoslav forces would have taken place.

Planned weapons configuration normally consisted of one to four Hellfire missiles, 440 rounds of 30mm ammunition, and M-261 2.75-inch rocket pods. By April 27, the task force had approximately 800 Hellfire missiles in Albania.[39] This configuration allowed the aircraft to carry an Extended Range Fuel System. Due to the vulnerability of this system to enemy fire, these wing tanks were to be used

---

[39]Unpublished Task Force Hawk Daily Situation Report, April 27, 1999.

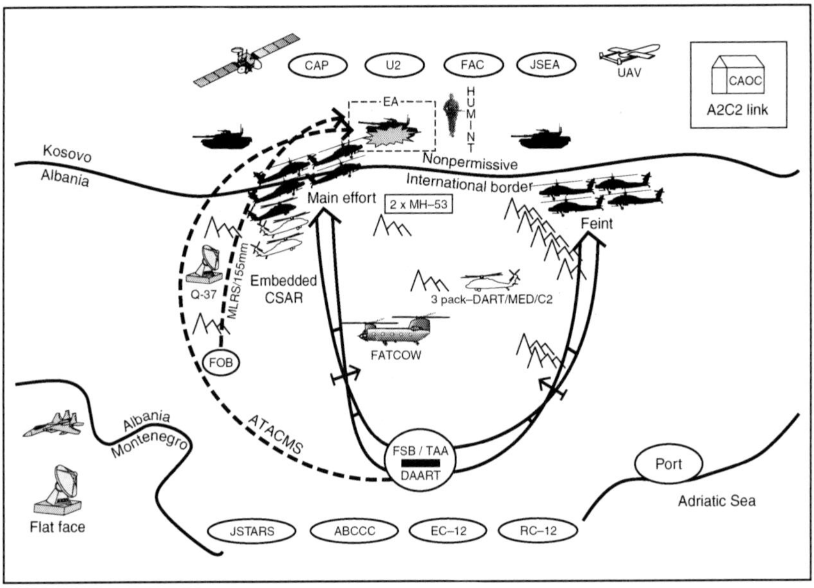

Figure 4.9—Task Force Hawk Deep-Attack Concept

only when it appeared that forward refueling points would not be feasible.

The Task Force developed detailed mission "go/no-go" and abort criteria. The "no go" criteria included:

- Target not approved.

- Mission rehearsal not completed.

- Key communications inoperative.

- Target and engagement area intelligence not current (more than four hours old from time of forward line of own troops crossing).

- Suppression of enemy air defenses not available for en route and in engagement area for known air defense positions.

- Weather less than 1,000-foot ceiling and two-mile in-flight visibility.

- Restricted operation zone not approved by the CAOC.[40]

- Combat search and rescue not approved by CAOC.

Had any of these "no go" criteria been met, a planned mission would not be launched. Once a mission was in progress, the abort criteria included the following:

- Combat loss of two aircraft in the attacking element of 4 or 5 AH-64s.

- Loss of communications from the executing elements with the Deep Operations Coordination Cell, command and control, or the Airborne Battle Command and Control Center.

- En route and engagement area weather less than 1,000-foot ceiling and two-mile in-flight visibility.

- Combat search and rescue elements must consist of at least one MH-60, Pavehawk, and one MH-53, Pavelow.

- Change of air mission commander occurs and mission success is compromised.

- The air mission commander thinks that the mission cannot be accomplished.[41]

Training and Rehearsals

TF Hawk mission rehearsal exercises started shortly after the Apaches arrived in Albania. The first daytime rehearsal in Albania took place on April 22 and the first night rehearsal on April 24. These rehearsals were essential to develop mission procedures and tactics and familiarize pilots with the unique terrain. Additionally, the flying conditions in Albania were difficult, with steep mountains that the aircraft had to negotiate at night.

---

[40]The restricted operation zone would assure that attack helicopter operations did not conflict with other operations by NATO aircraft in Kosovo air space.

[41]Interview with Task Force Hawk participant, October 20, 1999;"Task Force Hawk in Operation Allied Force."

The training objectives were to ensure that the air crews were validated in the following areas before missions were conducted: Deep Operations Coordination Cell procedures, fire support procedures, the mission command and control system, combat search and rescue, downed aircraft procedures, the ability to fly mission routes through the mountains, and the tactics to be employed in the engagement areas.[42]

During these mission rehearsal exercises, an Apache crashed on April 26, and another on May 5. Both crew members died in the May 5 accident.

Frequent rehearsals were conducted at Rinas. Rehearsals started with an intelligence update by the task force intelligence officer, followed by a detailed review of how a mission would be conducted, including operations at the engagement area under consideration. Air crews were able to rehearse missions with the aid of computer simulations that utilized high-resolution terrain imagery. Additionally, air crews were able to use the Air Mission Planning Simulator.

When first deployed, the Apache crews lacked training with night-vision goggles. Prior to the deployment to Albania, the Germany-based Apache battalions had relied on the aircraft's forward-looking infrared system (FLIR) for night flying. However, the FLIR was inadequate to support night navigation under the conditions prevailing in Albania, primarily because of the country's mountainous conditions. The integration of night-vision goggles was not a simple matter, requiring additional training in Albania. Since only one of the two Apache crewmen wears night-vision goggles, their use complicates coordination between the pilot and gunner. UH-60 support aircraft, which frequently accompanied AH-64 missions, did not have FLIR and had to rely solely on night-vision goggles.[43]

---

[42]General Clark described a "three-phased training plan: first, fly the Apaches to the border alone; second, assemble the complete package, fly to the border, and simulate the firing of the suppressive fires; third, assemble the complete package, fly to the border, and actually fire the suppressive fires, without bringing the Apaches across. Only then would we move to the real missions." Clark, *Waging Modern War*, pp. 279–280.

[43]"Task Force Hawk in Operation Allied Force"; "Operation Victory Hawk After Action Report"; interviews with Task Force Hawk participants, October 20, 1999, and February 4, 2000.

RAND *MR1406-4.10*

SOURCE: Defense Visual Information Center *(www.dodmedia.osd.mil)*.

Figure 4.10—Apaches Lifting Off for Mission Rehearsal Exercise

Forward Operating Base

After TF Hawk established itself in the immediate vicinity of the Rinas airport, plans were made to establish a forward operating base near Kcire close to the Albania-Kosovo border. This base, which was operational about May 1, provided a location for intelligence gathering and for the MLRS launchers to fire air defense suppression missions into Kosovo.

Located at the forward operating base were a portion of the MLRS battalion tactical operations center, one battery of MLRS launchers, a platoon of M-109A6 Paladin self-propelled howitzers, and a meteorological section. Since the forward operating base was roughly 100 kilometers from the main base at Rinas, it required its own force protection. This was provided by a dismounted infantry company, a platoon of M-2 Bradley Fighting Vehicles, a 120mm mortar section, an air defense section, a scout platoon, a military police platoon, engineers, intelligence personnel (including a ground surveillance radar), and logistics and medical personnel. A defensive perimeter was established at the forward operating base, since the only forces between it and the Albania-Kosovo border were elements of the ineffective Albanian army and KLA. Troops were rotated from the main body of TF Hawk at Rinas to the forward operating base. On May 15, for example, roughly 475 personnel were located at the forward operating base.[44]

Communications from the forward operating base to task force headquarters in Rinas were via satellite. As the task force prepared for attack helicopter missions into Kosovo, the MLRS and cannon firing platoons located at the forward operating base participated in rehearsals. The main mission of the firing elements at this base would have been air defense suppression in support of helicopter penetrations into southwestern Kosovo. To rehearse missions (permission for surface-to-surface fires into Kosovo was never granted), the MLRS battery, the Paladin platoon, and elements of the tactical operations center left the forward operating base and moved to forward firing positions close to the border. Infantry protection was provided for the firing elements. In addition to being the primary "fire base" for the MLRS and cannons tasked to support the planned helicopter missions into Kosovo, the forward operating base supported a Q-37 radar site located roughly 20 kilometers forward of the base.[45]

Integration with Air Operations and Targeting

TF Hawk operations were intended to become part of NATO's phased air operation. When the task force was declared mission capable and placed under the control of Joint Task Force Noble Anvil, air operations had been under way for 45 days. Any operations

---

[44]Unpublished Task Force Hawk Daily Situation Report, May 15, 1999.

[45]"Task Force Hawk in Operation Allied Force."

by Army attack helicopters and missiles had to be closely integrated with the ongoing fighter and bomber missions being flown into Kosovo.

The main mechanism for TF Hawk to interact with the CAOC in Vicenza was via the Battlefield Coordination Element, an Army organization under the command of a colonel who normally represents the Army Force or Land Component Commander at the Air Operations Center. The Army's European Battlefield Coordination Element had trained regularly with the Air Force before, but not directly with V Corps, since the Battlefield Coordination Element usually acts as a liaison for land component headquarters higher than a corps. This lack of familiarity meant that some time was required before the Deep Operations Coordination Cell and Battlefield Coordination Element were fully integrated.[46]

The Deep Operations Coordination Cell at Tiranë had to coordinate its proposed missions with the CAOC in Vicenza. As the time for a proposed mission approached, planning became much more detailed. Since TF Hawk required suppression of air defense and other support from fixed-wing aircraft, missions were planned and listed on the air tasking order. When helicopter missions were not flown, aircraft originally earmarked to support TF Hawk were reallocated to other missions. This process allowed the task force to plan missions and establish "place holders" on the air tasking order if approval to execute was received.

The rules of engagement presented particular challenges for suppression of enemy air defenses. Throughout Operation Allied Force, the rules of engagement were stringent. Following several incidents in April, when civilians were inadvertently killed, rules of engagement became even more restrictive. For fixed-wing aircraft, the general requirement was for an airborne forward air controller or pilot to confirm visually that no civilians were in the vicinity of a target before releasing ordnance. This requirement proved to be very difficult for suppression of enemy air defenses in support of helicopter operations. Had the Apaches crossed the border into Kosovo, they would have been exposed to threats from small-arms

---

[46]"Operation Victory Hawk After Action Report"; interview with Task Force Hawk participant, December 3, 1999.

fire, anti-aircraft guns, and shoulder-fired air defense missiles, all
present in large numbers in southwest Kosovo. Since these weapons
are difficult to locate before they fire, substantial suppressive fires
could have been required to cover large areas. The task force conducted detailed terrain analysis to determine feasible locations for air
defense weapons along the potential flight routes into Kosovo; nevertheless, considerable numbers of air defense weapons could have
been encountered along any of the routes into Kosovo. The restrictive rules of engagement, which required positive target identification to confirm that there were no civilians in the vicinity, were not
conducive to expending large amounts of firepower to suppress
enemy air defenses.[47] It should be noted that even with less restrictive ROE, the problem of locating and suppressing low-altitude
air defenses would have been difficult. Low-altitude systems, such as
anti-aircraft guns and shoulder-fired missiles, are generally passive,
nonemitting systems. When combined with their relatively small
size, these nonemitting weapons are easy to conceal. Additionally,
they were present in Kosovo in very large numbers—many hundreds
of anti-aircraft guns and shoulder-fired missiles were in the VJ units
operating in Kosovo.

Army counterfire radars and Hunter UAVs provided significant support in locating targets. Indeed, by late May, when it had become
apparent to the leadership of TF Hawk that their helicopters would
probably not be employed, the intelligence-collection efforts of the
task force shifted to identifying a daily "Top 10" target list for the
CAOC. Using their various intelligence systems, TF Hawk's Deep
Operations Coordination Cell focused on locating Yugoslav forces in
southwestern Kosovo and providing updated attack recommendations for the CAOC.[48] The "Top 10" list was updated twice daily. This
target list from TF Hawk became the basis for CAOC attack planning
against Yugoslav forces in southern Kosovo.[49] In addition to the daily
"Top 10" target recommendations, TF Hawk's Q-37s were observing

---

[47]"Operation Victory Hawk After Action Report"; interviews with Task Force Hawk
participant, October 20, 1999, and with U.S. European Command, November 12, 1999.

[48]General Clark notes that TF Hawk was also in regular contact with the Albanian
army, which in turn was monitoring the KLA, resulting in the passing of additional
targets to the CAOC. Clark, *Waging Modern War*, p. 329.

[49]"Task Force Hawk in Operation Allied Force."

the firing of Yugoslavian artillery and mortar units that were engaging the KLA in southwest Kosovo. As enemy artillery and mortar units were detected, the firing location was quickly transmitted to the CAOC for possible engagement by NATO aircraft. Figure 4.11 depicts the joint targeting process utilizing Army assets. One of the noteworthy points is the difference in time required to locate a target, pass that information, and then get a strike aircraft over that target. The Q-37 could pass targeting information to the CAOC in about 2 minutes; it took 3 hours to get a strike aircraft to the target area, plenty of time for the target to move to another area. The restrictive rules of engagement were a major factor in this, requiring positive identification of a target (and the absence of civilians) before ordnance could be dropped.

RAND *MR1406–4.11*

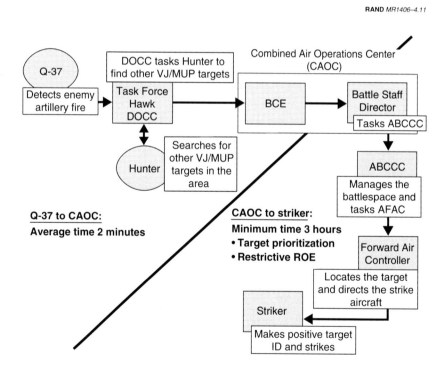

Figure 4.11—Joint Targeting Process

TASK FORCE HUNTER

Task Force Hunter was the Army's UAV detachment located in Macedonia. The Joint Chiefs of Staff approved Task Force Hunter on March 21, and it deployed shortly thereafter from the United States to Macedonia. The unit was required to become operational by April 5, with the initial mission of contributing to the protection of NATO forces located in Macedonia by conducting reconnaissance of Yugoslav forces located in southern Kosovo.

The initial Hunter capability was four aircraft equipped with electro-optical and infrared sensors (see Figure 4.12). Capable of operating at a maximum altitude of 15,000 feet with a mission radius of roughly 180 nautical miles, four Hunters could provide 12 hours of target coverage daily.

When TF Hawk deployed to Albania, Task Force Hunter provided liaison personnel to TF Hawk's headquarters. Hunter came under the operational control of TF Hawk on April 23. Task Force Hunter

RAND *MR1406-4.12*

SOURCE: *www.fas.org.*

Figure 4.12—Army Hunter UAV

became one of the most important sources of intelligence available to TF Hawk. Hunter missions were planned three days in advance and updated daily by TF Hawk's Deep Operations Coordination Cell. Once mission details were finalized, the liaison personnel located with the Deep Operations Coordination Cell would transmit mission details to the main body of Task Force Hunter in Macedonia, and the missions would be flown. No Hunter missions were flown from Albania.[50]

TF Hawk relied heavily on intelligence gathered from Task Force Hunter. As deep-attack missions were planned for the Apaches, UAVs that flew over southern Kosovo provided much of the data on the location of Yugoslav forces. As early as mid-April, Task Force Hunter was passing data from its missions to the CAOC. Hunter was locating high-priority targets such as surface-to-air missile sites and their associated infrastructure, and the data were relayed to the CAOC for attack. Hunter then provided battle damage assessment following the attack.[51] Toward the end of the campaign, Hunter missions were being flown at the specific request of the CAOC. Tasks performed by the UAVs included gathering intelligence, target acquisition, battle damage assessment, and area reconnaissance. These missions were not without risk. Several UAVs were lost due to malfunctioning and anti-aircraft fire.[52] Weather presented additional challenges, and some missions were cancelled due to bad weather. Additionally, icing of the unmanned aerial vehicles was a problem until mid-May.[53] The strength of Task Force Hunter eventually grew to approximately 130 personnel.[54]

---

[50]Unpublished Task Force Hawk Daily Situation Report, April 22–23, 1999.

[51]Unpublished Task Force Hawk Daily Situation Report, April 16–17, 1999.

[52]Unpublished Task Force Hawk Daily Situation Reports. For example, two Hunters were lost in crashes on May 19.

[53]Unpublished Task Force Hawk Daily Situation Report, April 22–23, 1999.

[54]Unpublished Task Force Hawk Daily Situation Reports; interview with Task Force Hawk participant, December 3, 1999; and "Operation Victory Hawk After Action Report."

WHY WASN'T TASK FORCE HAWK EMPLOYED IN KOSOVO?

Having gone to great effort to deploy TF Hawk, why did the United States decline to employ it? Ultimately, it was because decision-makers perceived the risks to outweigh the potential benefits. This cost-benefit imbalance was the result of several interrelated factors: vulnerability of the attack helicopters to low-altitude air defenses; restrictive rules of engagement that did not permit those air defenses to be suppressed by area fires; the large number of hard-to-locate low-altitude air defense systems; the dearth of lucrative targets to justify high-risk helicopter operations; and the sensitivity to crew and helicopter losses, magnified after two training accidents. Further-more, by the time TF Hawk was operational, NATO fixed-wing aircraft were flying many sorties and suffering no casualties at medium altitude.

The main threat to TF Hawk operations was posed by the numerous low-altitude air defense systems located in Kosovo. By the time TF Hawk was ready to conduct operations, the Yugoslav army had deployed several hundred anti-aircraft guns and shoulder-fired missiles in the province. Although the night-fighting capability of many of these weapons was limited, their sheer number made the low-altitude environment challenging. Additionally, the threat from infantry weapons fire (e.g., rifles, machine guns, and rocket-propelled grenades) could have been significant given the large number of Yugoslav troops in the province, most of them operating in small, dispersed groups. It should be noted that even at the start of Operation Allied Force, and well before TF Hawk was operational, the Yugoslav forces inside Kosovo had deployed large numbers of low-altitude air defense weapons.

The desire to keep NATO casualties as low as possible and the con-cern over casualties among the refugees in Kosovo further compli-cated the use of attack helicopters. Given the large numbers of low-altitude air defense systems in Kosovo, significant amounts of air defense suppression would have been required to assist deep-penetration missions by the helicopters. TF Hawk planners expected to employ the MLRS along the routes into and out of Kosovo. But the rules of engagement required positive identification of targets and thus precluded such anticipatory fires. If the rules of engagement were relaxed to allow heavy fires by the MLRS and these inadvertently fell on civilians, the entire NATO air operation could have been discredited and perhaps jeopardized.[55]

There were also not enough lucrative targets to justify attack helicopter operations. Even before Operation Allied Force began, Yugoslav forces in Kosovo were operating in small, highly dispersed elements. As a result, attack helicopters could have attacked only a few military vehicles at a time. Never did Yugoslav forces present a massed target of battalion or larger size—the type of target that deep-strike attack helicopter missions would normally be planned against. Many U.S. military leaders did not consider these limited targets of sufficient value to justify the increased risk.

Last, Washington's support for Apache operations seems to have eroded as a result of two crashes in training during late April and early May, the second crash taking the lives of both crew members.[56] In late May, General Clark made a request to employ the Apaches without crossing into Yugoslav territory, proposing that the Hellfire missiles be fired into Kosovo from the Albanian border. The request was subsequently denied on the grounds of insufficient targets and too much risk.[57]

CONTRIBUTIONS OF TASK FORCE HAWK

Although TF Hawk never fired a shot or crossed into Kosovo, it did contribute to the overall success of Operation Allied Force. Milosevic very likely viewed TF Hawk—and NATO forces in Macedonia—as precursors for an air-land invasion of Kosovo, if he successfully endured the air attack.

TF Hawk scouted routes from the port of Durrës to the Albania-Kosovo border. Engineering elements linked to the task force were improving the infrastructure to support the movement of heavy

---

[55]The degree of concern over collateral damage was exemplified in DoD guidance that enemy air defense positions be observed and verified up to a few hours prior to firing against those positions. General Clark believed that adhering to this requirement would make Apache missions extremely difficult to conduct. Clark, *Waging Modern War*, p. 304.

[56]Interview with U.S. European Command, November 12, 1999.

[57]Clark, *Waging Modern War*, pp. 321, 367.

forces in Albania. When hostilities ended, TF Hawk included important elements of V Corps headquarters, a maneuver brigade headquarters, a battalion-size mechanized task force, engineers, and a
reinforced light infantry battalion, all units that would have contributed to a larger ground attack force. Additionally, the MLRS and
artillery units in the task force represented an initial fire support
capability to support a ground invasion. Many more units would
have been required, but TF Hawk included many of the important
elements around which a larger force could have been assembled,
including a corps commander and his staff, had a ground offensive
been required to eject Yugoslav forces from Kosovo. It was General
Clark's view that "the force conveyed a powerful image of a ground
threat, and would have been its lead component."[58]

The presence of TF Hawk also probably helped reassure the Albanian
government of NATO's commitment to its defense and increased its
support for Operation Allied Force. The KLA was operating principally from Albania across the border into Kosovo. At any time, Yugoslav forces might have entered Albania in hot pursuit or in a more
deliberate operation to destroy KLA bases of support. The weak Albanian military had little ability to resist an attack, but TF Hawk
could have responded forcefully.

And while important air-land synergies were not realized due to the
absence of a ground maneuver force, TF Hawk's attack helicopters
and missiles were another threat that Yugoslav forces operating in
Kosovo had to plan to counter.

Operational and Tactical Contributions

TF Hawk intelligence assets and target development capabilities
assisted in locating Yugoslav forces in Kosovo. The TF Hawk Deep
Operations Coordination Cell provided a capability to process intelligence data and develop ground force targets. TF Hawk provided
intelligence data in support of Operation Allied Force through its
Q-37 Firefinder radars and the Hunter. Although the mountainous
terrain along the border limited the maximum range of the Q-37, the
radar was able to locate a large number of Yugoslav artillery pieces.

---

[58]Clark, *Waging Modern War,* p. 425.

Timely response of attack assets was the more daunting challenge. Additionally, TF Hawk's training exercises inside Albania contributed to intelligence collection.

The Q-37 Firefinder radars deployed in eastern Albania detected Yugoslav artillery and mortars firing on the KLA. Since surface-to-surface fires were prohibited, a system was devised to pass the data quickly from the Q-37 to the CAOC for allocation of air attack assets. Data gained from the Army radars contributed to some increase in the effectiveness of air attacks in the final weeks of the conflict. The challenge was to attack targets quickly enough. The time lag between locating the target and the arrival of an airborne forward air controller and then a strike aircraft was such that most targets had disappeared before strike aircraft were overhead.

The Army's Hunter unmanned aerial vehicles helped locate Yugoslav forces operating in southern and western Kosovo. Initially these data were used to help plan Army attack helicopter missions. Later, when it became clear that the Apaches would probably not be employed, the data from the Hunters were used to help develop a better picture of the enemy to assist the ongoing air attacks.

Chapter Five

ENFORCING THE PEACE

On June 12, 1999, NATO forces began entering Kosovo to conduct Operation Joint Guardian. The Kosovo Force (KFOR) continues to the present day. This chapter examines the planning and initial execution of Operation Joint Guardian and the U.S. contribution, Task Force Falcon.

PREPARATION FOR OPERATION JOINT GUARDIAN

The planning and preparation that eventually led to Operation Joint Guardian, better known as KFOR, underwent many changes. Planning for KFOR began in the summer of 1998 but was halted during the October crisis. Planning began again in the lead-up to the negotiations held in Rambouillet, France, in February 1999. When the Rambouillet negotiations failed to produce a political settlement to the crisis, Joint Guardian was shelved again. Instead, planning and coordination for Operation Allied Force accelerated, with the operation commencing on March 24.

The rapid conclusion of hostilities in early June refocused allied attention on Operation Joint Guardian. On June 9, NATO and Yugoslavia signed a Military Technical Agreement, which called for a phased withdrawal of all Yugoslav forces over an 11-day period and a simultaneous deployment of a NATO-led stabilization force.[1] U.S.,

---

[1] "Military-Technical Agreement Between the International Security Force (KFOR) and the Government of the Federal Republic of Yugoslavia and the Federal Republic of Serbia," June 9, 1999. This agreement and other detailed information about KFOR are available at *http://www.kforonline.com*.

NATO, and other forces conducted final coordination for the deployment of KFOR.

The surprise movement of Russian forces from Bosnia into the Pristina airport on June 10 caught NATO by surprise. General Clark requested that Lieutenant General (U.K.) Sir Michael Jackson, the KFOR commander, order the Russians to withdraw from the airport, but Jackson refused to act, instead informing his home government, which agreed that KFOR should not confront the Russians. The issue was later resolved without incident, but it illustrated the difference between a national chain of command, in which subordinates are normally expected to obey orders, and an alliance chain of command, in which senior commanders may appeal to their national command authorities.[2]

United Nations Security Council Resolution 1244

On June 10, the United Nations Security Council passed Resolution (UNSCR) 1244 authorizing the deployment of an international civil and military presence to Kosovo. In part, UNSCR 1244 demanded a political solution based on the general principles set forth by the G-8 Foreign Ministers on May 6, 1999, and contained in the Ahtisaari-Chernomyrdin Agreement of June 2, 1999: the full cooperation of Yugoslavia in the rapid implementation of the principles in the Military-Technical Agreement; an immediate and verifiable end to violence and repression in Kosovo; and a complete and verifiable phased withdrawal of all military, police, and paramilitary forces in Kosovo.[3] The UN was designated to lead the interim civil authority, later termed the United Nations Interim Administration in Kosovo (UNMIK).

UNSCR 1244 also set forth very specific guidelines for the international security presence. Responsibilities of KFOR included the following:

---

[2]A detailed account of the Pristina airfield episode and decisionmaking is in Clark, *Waging Modern War,* pp. 375–403.

[3]United Nations, UN Security Council Resolution 1244, S/RES/1244(1999), June 10, 1999. Available at *http://www.un.org/docs/scres/1999/99sc1244.htm.*

- Deterring renewed hostilities, enforcing the cease-fire, and both ensuring the withdrawal and preventing the return of Yugoslav military, police, and paramilitary forces;

- Demilitarizing the KLA and other armed Kosovar Albanian groups;

- Establishing a secure environment in which refugees and displaced persons could return home in safety, the international civil presence could operate, a transitional administration could be established, and humanitarian aid could be delivered;

- Ensuring public safety and order and supervising the removal of mines until the international civil presence could take over;

- Supporting the work of the international civil presence and coordinating closely with it;

- Conducting border monitoring duties; and

- Ensuring the protection of movement of itself, the international civil presence, and other international organizations.[4]

INITIAL OPERATIONS IN KOSOVO

The dramatic Russian gambit at Pristina caused NATO to accelerate its deployment into Kosovo. The first elements entered Kosovo on June 12. This deployment and the phased withdrawal of Yugoslav forces went smoothly. By June 20, all Yugoslav forces had departed Kosovo and KFOR was well established. The KLA was later disbanded, and many of its personnel joined the newly formed Kosovo Protection Corps.

Kosovo Force Structure and Disposition

The Kosovo Force is organized in five multinational brigades (MNB) as shown in Figure 5.1. The lead nations for these brigades are France (MNB North), Germany (MNB South), Italy (MNB West), the United Kingdom (MNB Central) and the United States (MNB East). Although brigades are responsible for a specific area of operation,

---

[4]Ibid.

they all fall under a single KFOR (NATO) chain of command. Also, in an important change from the NATO-led Stabilization Force operation in Bosnia, KFOR troops were allowed to cross brigade boundaries to participate in combined operations under the Joint Guardian Operations Plan. This planned capability could have given KFOR great flexibility in responding to crises. Unfortunately, however, several national commands withdrew this authority in early 2000 when faced with incidents of ethnic conflict and violence in the flashpoint northern city of Kosovska Mitrovica.

RAND *MR1406-5.1*

Figure 5.1—KFOR Multinational Brigades

Entry of Task Force Falcon

The United States had pledged a total of 7,000 troops as part of Operation Joint Guardian. In addition to the U.S. forces, the 501st Mechanized Infantry Battalion (Greece), the 18th Air Assault Battalion (Poland) and the 13th Tactical Group (Russia) established positions in the U.S. sector known as MNB East. The U.S. and other forces (with the exception of the Russian unit) were designated Task Force Falcon.

The U.S. forces that moved into Kosovo included elements from TF Hawk and the 26th Marine Expeditionary Unit. Soldiers from Task Force 2-505, which had augmented TF Hawk in Albania, rapidly secured the location outside Urosevac where Camp Bondsteel, the headquarters for MNB East, was later located. Task Force 2-505 was a battalion-sized task force made up of three light infantry companies, one mechanized infantry company, and one tank company, artillery elements, and other combat support and combat service support assets. Initial operations focused on ensuring the withdrawal of all Yugoslav forces in accordance with the Military-Technical Agreement and establishing a secure environment. With a strong force posture and frequent presence patrols, Task Force 2-505 encountered little armed resistance or opposition.

The 26th Marine Expeditionary Unit (MEU) deployed as part of Task Force Falcon on June 14, 1999. The MEU established its position in the eastern half of the American sector, with its operations centered on the principal city in that part of the sector, Gnjilane. Headquarters for the 26th MEU, Battalion Landing Team 3/8, and Marine Service Support Group 26 were established at the forward operations base, Camp Montieth.[5] The operational environment oscillated between periods of intense activity and lulls. Although the Marines focused on force protection, they also conducted some civil affairs activities. Marine leaders met with local officials and occasionally

---

[5]Nathan S. Lowrey, "Peacekeeping Operations in Kosovo: The 26th MEU During Operation Joint Guardian," *Marine Corps Gazette*, December 1999, pp. 57–63. See also a series of articles on the "Kosovo Commitment" in *Marine Corps Gazette*, November 1999.

provided direct humanitarian assistance, ranging from the investigation of criminal activity to the relocation of families.[6]

Initial Tasks

KFOR's immediate task was to ensure that Yugoslav forces complied with the timeline for their withdrawal contained in the Military-Technical Agreement. This task required KFOR to deploy quickly into the province to prevent a security vacuum in contested areas. KFOR elements met with Yugoslav military liaison teams in Pristina and elsewhere to ensure proper transfer of military authority in the region. Yugoslav forces completed their withdrawal by June 20, the deadline in the Military-Technical Agreement.

KFOR also provided humanitarian assistance to internally displaced persons and members of ethnic groups remaining in their homes but lacking basic supplies, and to refugees in countries bordering Kosovo who wanted to return to their homes. International organizations, especially the United Nations High Commissioner for Refugees, took over this task as soon as they became operational in the province. KFOR established Civil-Military Cooperation Centers in each national sector to coordinate military assistance to humanitarian operations.

From the outset, KFOR assumed responsibility for the protection of ethnic minorities and historic cultural sites. Of particular concern were Serbs who chose to remain in Kosovo. This remaining Serb population is largely concentrated in the French and American zones along the southern border of Serbia.

KFOR also disarmed the KLA. KFOR representatives signed an "Undertaking of Demilitarization and Transformation by the KLA" on June 20. This agreement provided for a "cease-fire by the KLA, their disengagement from the zones of conflict, subsequent demilitarization and reintegration into civil society."[7] This was scheduled to occur within 90 days. KFOR units immediately established

---

[6] Lowrey, "Peacekeeping Operations in Kosovo," p. 59.

[7]"Undertaking of Demilitarisation and Transformation by the Kosovo Liberation Army," June 20, 1999, available from *http://www.kforonline.com.*

weapons storage sites throughout the province to provide a collection and safeguard point for the storage of all weapons requiring turn-in in accordance with the June 20 agreement. KFOR also monitored the wearing of KLA uniforms and insignia. Although the KLA was initially slow in turning in its weapons, the numbers increased significantly as the deadline approached. By September 20, General Jackson certified that the force had completed its process of demilitarization and ceased to display KLA insignia.[8]

The Kosovo Protection Corps was established on September 21, 1999. Under the direction of the KFOR and UNMIK, the Kosovo Protection Corps has authority to provide disaster response, conduct search and rescue, provide humanitarian assistance, assist in demining, and contribute to rebuilding infrastructure and communities. It has no role, however, in defense, law enforcement, riot control, internal security, or any other task involved in the maintenance of law and order. The maximum strength of the Kosovo Protection Corps is 5,000 (3,000 active, 2,000 reserve).[9] All ethnic groups are supposed to participate, but few Serbs have sought to join.

CHALLENGES FACING KFOR

In addition to facing a complex operating environment in which ethnic tensions remained high and vengeful Kosovar Albanians attacked Serbs and other minorities, KFOR suffered from internal problems. It has had difficulty maintaining required troop levels. At various times, several troop-contributing countries have unilaterally withdrawn forces to meet needs elsewhere. As a result, KFOR troop levels have fluctuated significantly since June 1999. During the February 2000 crisis in Mitrovica, for example, KFOR had no more than 37,000 troops, 12,000 fewer than anticipated in the original op-

---

[8]Statement by Lieutenant General Ceku, Chief of Staff, Kosovo Liberation Army, September 20, 1999. Available at *http://www.kforonline.com*.

[9]The Kosovo Protection Corps, Commander, Kosovo Force's Statement of Principles; UNMIK/RE/1999/8, On the Establishment of the Kosovo Protection Corps. Available at *http://www.kforonline.com*.

erational plan.[10]   Several countries sent reinforcements, but KFOR still remains below its planned strength.

Little coordination occurs among the multinational brigades.   Despite early NATO efforts to give the commander of KFOR control over all forces in Kosovo, each national force still goes its own way.   For example, there are currently six information operation plans in Kosovo: one KFOR plan and one for each of the five MNBs.[11]   As a result, information operations are fragmented and less effective than a unified effort might be.

More important, the KFOR commander cannot draw forces from one brigade area to reinforce another as the situation might require. Contributors have refused to implement the mechanism originally intended to provide him this authority.   When, for example, during the February 2000 crisis, Jackson directed U.S. forces to reinforce in the French sector, the United States insisted that these forces return to their own sector.[12]   The stated reason for this decision was that moving forces would jeopardize the U.S. position in MNB East, but it dramatically illustrated the limits of NATO control over forces in Kosovo.   At present, only U.K. forces are readily available to the commander of KFOR for deployment outside their brigade sector.[13]

The Law and Order Problem

KFOR and UNMIK have focused on maintaining law and order because instability has continually bedeviled the international effort in Kosovo.   While UNMIK is the sole legitimate political authority in Kosovo, former KLA officials or armed criminal elements have real power in much of the province.   Moreover, neither UNMIK nor KFOR were adequately configured or staffed.   UNMIK, in particular, has

---

[10]Elizabeth Becker, "Not Enough Troops in Kosovo, NATO Says," *The New York Times*, February 26, 2000.

[11]Interview with government contractor on assignment in Kosovo, Washington, D.C., August 2, 2000.

[12]Richard Beeston, Michael Evans, and Ian Brodie, "Pentagon Withholds Mitrovica Unit," *London Times*, February 29, 2000, and Robert Burns, "US to Limit Kosovo Patrols," Associated Press, February 29, 2000.

[13]Institute for National Security Studies (INSS), *Peace Operations Forum*, Washington, D.C.: National Defense University, April 12, 2000.

been understaffed and underfunded throughout its existence, with over 50 percent of its positions unoccupied and barely enough funding to cover its payroll. Nor does KFOR have sufficient troops to accomplish the objectives outlined in UNSCR 1244. In view of these limitations, UNMIK and KFOR changed their goal in November 1999 from multiethnicity to peaceful coexistence of the various ethnic groups.[14]

The United Nations civilian police effort was slow to make a significant impact in Kosovo. As of November 22, 1999, 1,974 UN officers were deployed in all five regions of the province and at four border crossings. They patrolled high-risk areas alone and jointly with KFOR troops. But UN police forces had difficulty establishing a strong presence outside of Pristina. Many of the international police were poorly prepared for their duties. For example, the entire 100-man Nepalese contingent had to return home because some were not properly equipped and others spoke no English.[15] The UNMIK Head of Mission requested 6,000 civilian police officers, but recruitment has never approached this level.[16]

The departure of the Yugoslav police and international reluctance to use former KLA soldiers caused a vacuum in indigenous law enforcement. UNMIK established a police academy to fill this void through training a new multiethnic Kosovo Police Service. This academy was initially successful. In 2000, the first four classes had 15 percent ethnic minority enrollment (Serb, Roma, Turk, and Muslim Slav) and 20 percent of the cadets were women, a very high percentage considering the patriarchal nature of Kosovar society. Moreover, there was only one incident in the first seven months that involved a dispute between ethnic groups.[17] Graduates from the academy operate under supervision from UN international police "field training officers." Unfortunately, most of these officers have little training in

---

[14]Ibid., remarks by former UNMIK officials.

[15]Andrew Roche, "Law and Order Is Kosovo's Achilles Heel," Reuters, December 27, 1999.

[16]"Starting from Scratch in Kosovo: The Honeymoon Is Over," International Crisis Group, *ICG Balkans Report No. 83*, December 10, 1999, pp. 4–5.

[17]INSS, *Peace Operations Forum*, April 12, 2000.

mentoring and little familiarity with the region.[18] It remains to be seen how effective the new Kosovo Police Service will become in the long term.

The biggest obstacle to law and order in Kosovo, however, is the continued presence of armed extremists. Although the KLA was disarmed, its members retained thousands of individual weapons. Moreover, some Albanian members of the Kosovo Protection Corps have engaged in forcible evictions, extortion, and interrogations.[19] Kosovar Serb elements continue to receive financial and other support from Belgrade.

U.S. Emphasis on Force Protection in Kosovo

Force protection remains the first priority for U.S. forces in Kosovo. U.S. forces are based principally in Camp Bondsteel near Urosevac and in Camp Montieth near Gnjilane. These heavily fortified camps serve as the bases for U.S. operations throughout the sector. Vehicles leaving Camps Bondsteel or Montieth had to travel in convoys with vehicular-mounted weapons (e.g., .50-caliber machine gun). The morale of the soldiers in the field remained generally high, although some were frustrated by the lack of progress.[20]

U.S. forces also focus on stopping the flow of Kosovar Albanian weapons and guerrillas into Serbia. U.S. forces have raided suspected training bases and have confiscated weapons destined to support an ongoing Albanian insurgency in southern Serbia.[21] Still, the U.S. military's strong emphasis on force protection has greatly inhibited this type of action on a large-scale basis.

---

[18]"Starting Over from Scratch in Kosovo," p. 5.

[19]INSS, *Peace Operations Forum*, April 12, 2000.

[20]Interview with government contractor on assignment in Kosovo, Washington, D.C., August 2, 2000.

[21]Richard Mertens, "Keeping Order on Kosovo Border," *Christian Science Monitor*, March 17, 2000, p. 6.

KOSOVO IN CONTRAST TO BOSNIA

The Kosovo Force is a NATO-led peace enforcement operation comparable to the Stabilization Force in Bosnia-Herzegovina. Both are tasked to prevent the reemergence of conflict between the former warring parties. But in at least four aspects, the two operations differ greatly.

First, under UNSCR 1244, KFOR has a much broader mandate than does the Stabilization Force. KFOR's mission is not only to provide security, but also to maintain law and order until UNMIK can assume responsibility. NATO forces in Bosnia have no such responsibility under the General Framework Agreement for Peace in Bosnia and Herzegovina, better known as the Dayton Agreement.[22] The military's responsibilities were much more closely circumscribed, confining it to strictly military tasks. The military could assist civilian agencies and organizations, but only "within the limits of its assigned principal tasks."[23] Thus, during the first year of the international presence in Bosnia there was a constant tension between the military and civilian efforts. This condition improved over time as the security situation stabilized in Bosnia and especially once the majority of the military tasks had been accomplished.

Second, the conclusion to the conflict in Kosovo differs greatly from that in Bosnia. In Bosnia, the Dayton Agreement at least outlined a political settlement, and the Office of the High Representative was not expected to assume responsibility for civil government. However, the intransigence of the former warring parties led the UN Office of the High Representative to take a more intrusive role than expected. In Kosovo, there was no political settlement. Indeed, the political status of Kosovo was left unresolved. Almost all Kosovar Albanians want independence, but the international community has thus far refused to countenance that possibility. NATO fears that an independent Kosovo would cause instability in Macedonia, which has a large Albanian minority, and set a poor precedent for Bosnia.

Third, there was much more law and order in postwar Bosnia than in Kosovo. In Bosnia, the ethnic groups had legal systems and police

---

[22]See *http://www.ohr.int/gfa/gfa-home.htm* for the full text of the Dayton Agreement.

[23]General Framework Agreement for Peace in Bosnia and Herzegovina, Annex IA.

forces in operation. When NATO forces arrived, there were established authorities, although not always ones that NATO wished to continue unaltered. In Kosovo, by contrast, there was no civil authority after Yugoslav forces withdrew, other than the KLA, which had to be disbanded.

Finally, in Bosnia, the various ethnic groups spoke the same language and were often intermingled until the war largely separated them. In Kosovo, however, the ethnic demographics are quite different. Kosovar Albanians and Serbs speak different languages and traditionally have not intermingled.[24] As a result, there was little basis for the multiethnic government initially set as UNMIK's goal. Moreover, the wide-scale "ethnic cleansing" that occurred during Operation Allied Force has left so much fear and hatred as to practically preclude multiethnic cooperation for the foreseeable future.

---

[24]Samuel Berger, Assistant to the President for National Security Affairs, remarks at the United States Institute of Peace, Washington, D.C., September 30, 1999.

Chapter Six

CONCLUSION

The 1998–1999 crisis with Yugoslavia and Operation Allied Force provide rich experiences to draw on when considering future operations and force structure requirements. An important caveat is that all such events have their own unique strategic political context and operational military challenges. That said, a number of important issues arose that need to be considered as part of ongoing efforts to better prepare the U.S. military for future military operations.

THE LEVERAGE DERIVED FROM AN AIR-LAND CAMPAIGN APPROACH

Perhaps the most important observation is on the level of joint and multinational operations. Integration of national and allied military assets into a joint campaign presents an adversary with a range of challenges and threats that are likely to be far more difficult (and compelling) than anything possible using a single service or medium. In this sense, despite its many successes, Operation Allied Force demonstrated the strategic deficiencies of not taking a joint approach to a political-military conflict. By removing the forced-entry option from consideration in mid-1998, NATO robbed itself of a high-leverage threat that would certainly have caused Milosevic to reach a much more unfavorable estimate of the consequences of not reaching a political solution to the Kosovo crisis. Milosevic was therefore not presented with a compelling military threat in the run-up to Operation Allied Force and may have been encouraged to defy NATO and risk a battle of time and wills.

Once Operation Allied Force began, the absence of a credible joint force option ceded the initiative to Belgrade. Belgrade's decision to accelerate the ethnic cleansing was undertaken in recognition that NATO had virtually no ability to stop it by military means. Therefore the cleansing operation would have the time to exert political pressure on the weaker neighboring states (and by extension on NATO's resolve) while the alliance struggled with expanding its air-only operation. Furthermore, at the operational level, by not presenting Serb ground forces in Kosovo with an opposing ground threat, there was no need for those forces to concentrate to defend. As the evidence shows, the fielded forces survived NATO air strikes largely intact, due in no small part to their ability to remain dispersed. This same dispersion also became a powerful argument against employing the Apache attack helicopters. Given all this and the ever-present uncertainty over Russia's role, it was not unreasonable for Milosevic to conclude he could outlast and ultimately cause NATO to stand down.

There were of course powerful political reasons why mounting such an integrated joint campaign was not possible in this specific conflict. And there were advantages to deciding to conduct an air effort alone. As the one course of action with unanimous consent, it helped keep the NATO alliance together. It allowed NATO to begin operations promptly after Rambouillet, rather than waiting months to prepare for ground operations. It allowed great latitude and flexibility in targeting. It caused few casualties—only two aircraft shot down and no pilots lost—an important consideration for powers that had no vital interests at stake in the conflict. But despite these very real advantages, the consequences of not preparing for a fully integrated joint campaign are now apparent as well. When facing resistance to major military operations in the future, decisionmakers need to assess the political and military consequences of *not* undertaking an integrated joint approach to achieving their objectives. Senior military leaders need to apprise their civilian counterparts of the various risks of lesser alternatives.

JOINT "AIR-ONLY" OPERATIONS

Despite the compelling reasons to conduct integrated air-land operations, political conditions and constraints (as well as operational military realities in some instances) may preclude this preferred approach. Various forms of "air-only" or "deep fires only" operations may be adopted instead. Even under these circumstances, there is great value in using a joint approach and close partnership among the services from the outset to maximize the effectiveness of such operations. To attack enemy land forces more successfully, for example, air forces need insight into land force operations that their colleagues in sister services can provide. This was realized in the latter weeks of Operation Allied Force as TF Hawk's assets and expertise were integrated into the air operation. But it took time to bring about this integration, owing to the lack of a joint approach from the outset and the need to improvise procedures. Several steps should be considered to more effectively exploit the synergies of air and ground forces if faced with similarly constrained contingencies in the future.

Designation of a Land Component Commander

Even when substantial land forces are not involved, there should be a land component commander to help conduct intelligence preparation of the battlefield and to plan for use of land forces on a contingency basis.

No land component commander was designated during Operation Allied Force.[1] The commander of TF Hawk assumed some but not all of a land component commander's responsibilities. Admiral James O. Ellis, serving as Commander, Allied Forces Southern Europe, and Commander, Joint Task Force Noble Anvil, had no land component commander. In Ellis's opinion, it was a mistake not to have designated one:

---

[1] In his account, General Clark discusses the possible candidates and the difficulties they posed: General Montgomery Meigs, Commander, U.S. Army Europe, was a logical choice but was heavily committed in Bosnia; Michael Jackson, the British three-star then in charge of the ACE Rapid Reaction Corps (ARRC) based in Macedonia, would have posed the problem of a non-American commanding U.S. forces that might well be the largest ground force for an offensive; Lieutenant General Jay Hendrix was consumed by Task Force Hawk; and Admiral James Ellis had existing responsibilities both as the U.S. naval component commander and as overall operational commander in the NATO chain of command. Clark decided to defer the appointment. Clark, *Waging Modern War*, p. 283.

The lack of a Land Component Commander was doctrinally flawed and operationally dangerous. Having 5,000–6,000 troops on the ground in the Balkans and no LCC commander to provide oversight for the Joint Force Commander created a complex, confusing and potentially dangerous situation. The JFC was left without valuable expertise on the land component aspect (e.g., training, qualifications, contingency, operations, logistics, force protection, etc.). It also increased confusion by complicating planning and impeding an efficient operational chain of command.[2]

A land component commander can provide valuable assistance in targeting fielded forces. U.S. Air Force targeters are trained to develop targets focusing on an enemy's war-making potential and to help develop a full range of targets in joint operations. They are not trained, nor need they be trained, to plan attacks on fielded forces without help from Army and Marine Corps planners who have expert knowledge of land operations. There is no need to duplicate in the Air Force capabilities that already exist in the Army and Marine Corps. A land component commander would increase the effectiveness of air operations against fielded forces by bringing expert knowledge and resources to the associated problems of reconnaissance, targeting, and battle damage assessment.

The Joint Chiefs of Staff and the services should strengthen doctrine to recommend designation of a land component commander even when friendly land forces are absent from the area of operations or marginally involved. In addressing the Joint Force Commander's approach to operations, current joint doctrine states, "it *may* be useful to establish functionally oriented commanders responsible for the major operations."[3] Given the circumstances encountered in Operation Allied Force, stronger language on the importance of designating a land component commander in future operations is warranted. Therefore joint and service doctrine should note that when a unified commander prepares for such operations, he would normally designate a land component commander to advise the joint commander.

---

[2]Letter correspondence from Admiral Ellis to coauthor Walter Perry at RAND, December 2000.

[3]Italics added. See *Doctrine for Joint Operations*, Joint Pub 3-0, February 1, 1995, p. III-14.

Sensor-to-Shooter Response Time

Sensor-to-shooter response time should be shortened. It is often too long to engage fleeting targets successfully due to cumbersome control arrangements and the tendency to transmit reconnaissance data through service channels.

During Operation Allied Force, response times varied from tens of minutes to several hours, making the reconnaissance data of questionable value or useless for the shooter. Streamlined procedures can reduce response times, sometimes dramatically, but fundamental improvement demands a new concept. The Joint Staff and services should consider promoting a ground-based counterland control center with the responsibility for dynamically tasking reconnaissance means, fusing reconnaissance data to support targeting, and controlling shooters during tactical engagements. It might be located on a ship, on an airborne platform, or on land. If located on land, it would be easily expandable and defendable. Such a center would be jointly manned with representation from all services contributing to the joint effort.[4]

At the same time, it must be recognized that highly restrictive rules of engagement, while politically necessary, limit the effectiveness of even the best sensor-to-shooter linkages. In the case of Operation Allied Force, the requirements for "eyes on target" to minimize the risks of collateral damage frequently negated the utility of rapid targeting data, such as that provided by TF Hawk's Q-37 radars. Any future sensor-to-shooter architecture and associated procedures should be designed to operate as effectively as possible under these constrained conditions.

Joint Doctrine for Attack Helicopter Operations

Experience with TF Hawk revealed a gap in joint doctrine regarding attack helicopter operations in the absence of friendly land forces.

---

[4]These concepts are more fully developed in Alan Vick, Richard Moore, Bruce Pirnie, and John Stillion, *"Aerospace Operating Against Elusive Ground Targets,"* Santa Monica, CA: RAND, MR-1398-AF, 2001.

The joint commander, Admiral Ellis, and the AFSOUTH air component commander, General Short, did not fully appreciate how attack
helicopters could contribute to the air operation. Admiral Ellis later
remarked: "I fully agree that there was a lack of joint understanding
of attack helicopter operations and their incorporation as TF Hawk.
Doctrine for attack helicopters exists, but not for the situation in
which we found ourselves."[5]

Army doctrine addresses attack helicopters in deep attack, but it
envisions these operations as part of a combined arms team that
includes maneuver ground elements and artillery. In the case of TF
Hawk, several elements of the combined arms team were absent,
especially ground maneuver forces. Moreover, doctrine envisions
deep attack taking place in an area of operations where the land
component commander is the supported commander, which was
not the TF Hawk experience.

In the future, the Army's attack helicopters and the MLRS might well
be employed again in the absence of large land forces, either in pre-
dominately air operations or in the initial phase of a full campaign.
The Joint Staff and the services should refine doctrine to address
such employment and also include this use of deep-attack assets in
training and exercises.

PLANNING FOR MAJOR POLITICAL CONSTRAINTS ON
FUTURE MILITARY OPERATIONS

Operation Allied Force exhibited oft-remarked characteristics of
post–Cold War military operations: aims driven by humanitarian
concerns, aversion to friendly casualties, and restrictive rules of engagement. It also exemplified a U.S. tendency toward relying on air
power alone.

Characteristic Restraints

As in many other post–Cold War military operations, NATO's military
intervention in Kosovo was strongly influenced by humanitarian

---

[5]Letter correspondence from Admiral Ellis to coauthor Walter Perry at RAND,
December 2000.

concerns, to stop violence committed by the Yugoslav government against a despised minority. But the intervening governments had few political, military, or economic interests at stake. Presumably as a consequence, they were not willing to risk the casualties usually associated with decisive land operations. Restrictive rules of engagement, which were especially notable during the Kosovo conflict, are a further implication of humanitarian aims. It would have appeared hypocritical (and moreover have been illegal) had NATO inflicted great suffering on the Serb and Albanian populations when its own aims were humanitarian. It seems reasonable to conclude that many future operations will exhibit these same characteristics.

Tendency to Rely on Air Power

Operation Allied Force was one more example of a pronounced U.S. tendency to rely on air power in the Balkans. The Clinton Administration's first major initiative was to promote "lift and strike," a proposal strongly rejected by the European allies who already had forces on the ground. Air power was used to prevent Yugoslav combat aircraft from flying over Bosnia, to support UN forces deployed in Bosnia, and to enforce the so-called safe areas, most notably in Operation Deliberate Force. At the same time, the United States used air power to coerce Iraq through decade-long enforcement of no-fly zones. The overwhelming superiority of U.S. air forces, especially their ability to operate for extended periods in hostile air space with few casualties, makes such a strategy feasible. But these operations also imply limited target sets and restrictive rules of engagement that may prevent unfolding the full potential of air power, and inure an opponent to the effects of air power. Moreover, air power, for all its flexibility and precision, often cannot stop those activities the United States is most anxious to prevent, such as the "ethnic cleansing" of Kosovo.

The same applies to the air power of attack helicopters. TF Hawk faced highly restrictive rules of engagement that directly contributed to the decision not to employ the Apaches. The doctrinal use of massed fires to suppress enemy air defense ran into the competing objective to minimize civilian casualties. But the inability to use massed fires in turn drove up the vulnerability of the Apaches. And that greater vulnerability was in direct tension with yet a third objective, keeping aircraft and crew losses as close to zero as possible.

IMPROVING MILITARY PLANNING

The Kosovo conflict demonstrated the prudence and utility of comprehensive military planning, even for operations that exceed current political will.

NATO and the United States began Operation Allied Force with plans that did not extend much beyond a few days of air strikes. They had to improvise an extended air operation and still later develop plans for ground operations. The alliance members may tend to equate planning with intent and therefore resist planning operations they have not yet decided to conduct. In contrast, the United States routinely plans operations simply out of prudence. The United States should encourage NATO to plan more comprehensively for its out-of-area commitments. It would be preferable to do so in peacetime, before a crisis ensues, to allow military contingency planning to take place outside of a politically charged atmosphere. Failing this, the United States should plan comprehensively through its own channels, so that it will be better prepared to support the alliance or to act unilaterally if necessary. In the case of Kosovo, the United States should have anticipated that Milosevic might be intransigent and planned for an extended effort. Moreover, it should have planned at least conceptually for ground operations, even if they appeared politically infeasible at the time. As demonstrated by the Kosovo conflict, political will changes over time in response to new situations. Senior military authorities should convey to high-level decisionmakers the advantages of planning well prior to events and the risks of not planning.

The Army's Title 10 Planning Responsibilities

Because a "ground option" was foreclosed at the start of Operation Allied Force, ground planning was deferred and therefore lagged considerably behind air planning. The geographic Commander-in-Chief has clear responsibility for operational planning, but General Clark also had to contend with the many evolving political and military tensions within NATO and the imperative to manage them to keep the alliance together. His latitude to conduct ground planning was highly constrained. Furthermore, he and his staff faced a rapidly evolving situation in which compressed planning time limited the consideration of alternative courses of action and the operational details of using other military assets such as the Apaches.

The Army should consider establishing a contingency analysis cell to explore possible contingencies and identify operational constraints consistent with its Title 10 responsibilities in support of combatant commanders' requirements. The Army should develop methods for measuring the effect of various political and military constraints on deployment, sustainment, and employment of Army units. These methods would have two objectives: (1) to identify in advance alternative concepts of operations and force packages best suited to mission success under posited political and military constraints; and (2) to lay out more clearly and systematically the operational consequences for mission success of various constraints to clarify the acceptable range and tradeoffs among the constraints, risk to the force, and to mission success. Both of these peacetime objectives would be used to better support the CINC and the Army Chief of Staff in a crisis. They would also allow the Army to make the most of its ability to create and tailor task forces best suited to CINC operational conditions. They would complement the physical transformation of the force by providing more agile and responsive planning, supplying the CINC and Army Chief of Staff with a range of options that take best advantage of the Army's evolving capabilities.

NEED FOR EXPANDED GROUND-FORCE OPTIONS

The Army needs to offer national decisionmakers more viable options earlier in contingencies. Clearly, it needs to become more expeditionary at force levels lower than corps and full divisions. The usual requirement is one or two combat brigades within a task force that contains a wide variety of units normally found at higher echelons. Being more expeditionary should embrace the Army's full range of forces, including its heavy armor. Depending on the situation, the Army also has to argue convincingly either that it can gain decisive results at very low casualty rates (as it did during the Persian Gulf War) or that the better outcome would justify the increased risk of casualties. In Kosovo, for example, the Army would have to show

how, in close cooperation with superior air forces, Army forces could drive Yugoslav units out of the province quickly and with acceptable risk of friendly casualties.

DISPARITIES IN COALITION CAPABILITIES

Operation Allied Force highlighted disparities between U.S. and NATO forces so substantial as to create an impression that NATO was merely cover for an essentially U.S. effort. In view of declining European defense budgets, some disparities may even widen, but others could be fruitfully addressed.

Disparities were apparent in space-based surveillance, large-deck carrier operations, strategic airlift, radar-defeating stealth, mid-altitude reconnaissance with unmanned aerial vehicles, strike capabilities in reduced visibility, and precision strike at standoff ranges. The NATO members have successfully developed major items of equipment through common programs, especially aircraft such as the Tornado, but they continue to develop much equipment on a national basis, especially highly expensive items required for force projection. As a result, the United States has capabilities in such areas as space-based surveillance, large-deck carrier operations, strategic airlift, and radar-defeating stealth that appear unaffordable for the alliance. In other areas, such as mid-altitude reconnaissance with unmanned aerial vehicles, improved strike in poor visibility, and precision strike at standoff ranges, concerted effort might overcome or mitigate the disparities. In some areas, price may decline as technology matures. For example, the U.S.-developed Joint Direct Attack Munition and Joint Standoff Weapon are relatively inexpensive, compared with earlier systems.

NEED FOR INCREASED ARMY CAPABILITY TO CONDUCT CIVIL POLICE TASKS

The civil police tasks given to KFOR under UNSCR 1244 have significant implications for future peace operations. Although the U.S. Army is not ideally organized, trained, and equipped to conduct these tasks, it is probable that it will be called on to conduct similar missions in future peace operations. Therefore, the Army needs to consider ways to conduct these tasks effectively while minimizing the negative effects on combat readiness. Other countries have federal police units or paramilitary forces ideally suited for riot control and other missions that fall between the capabilities of military and police forces. No such units or organizations exist in the United States. To meet this need, for its part the Army could increase the number of military police units.

FINAL THOUGHTS

Perhaps more than anything, the Kosovo conflict highlighted both the importance of multinational military operations and the challenges they present. The future is likely to be characterized by conflicts in which political imperatives call for the United States to act as part of a larger political-military alliance or coalition. Yet the many benefits derived from multinational participation are often accompanied by increased complexity and a diversity of perspectives on how best to conduct military operations, as well as sometimes sharp differences over the costs and benefits of various courses of action. Skillful military leaders and planners will seek to anticipate possible constraints and be prepared to adapt to them if necessary.

The complexities of multinational operations also place an added premium on U.S. joint force integration. Beyond maximizing combat synergies, the joint force approach provides a wider array of military options to deal with unforeseen political-military conditions encountered in alliance and coalition environments. In this sense it is also a force multiplier.

As force providers and experts in land warfare, the Army has Title 10 responsibilities to ensure that its forces and planning bring to bear the requisite flexibility and considered range of options in both cases. Doing so will help ensure that the advantages of multinational operations are fully realized in the future.

LIST OF INDIVIDUALS CONSULTED

Senior Officials

Listed with rank at time of interview and by positions held during Operation Allied Force

General (USA) Wesley K. Clark, Supreme Allied Commander Europe and Commander in Chief, U.S. European Command

General (USA, retired) Dennis J. Reimer, Chief of Staff, U.S. Army

General (USA) Montgomery C. Meigs, Commander, U.S. Army Europe

Admiral (USN) James O. Ellis, Commander, Allied Forces Southern Europe; Commander in Chief, U.S. Naval Forces Europe; and Commander, Joint Task Force Noble Anvil

The Honorable Bernard Rostker, Under Secretary of the Army

Lieutenant General (USA) John W. Hendrix, Commanding General, V Corps, and Commander, Task Force Hawk

Lieutenant General (USAF) Michael C. Short, Commander, Allied Air Forces Southern Europe, and Commander, 16th Air Force

Lieutenant General (USA) Donald L. Kerrick, Deputy Assistant to the President for National Security Affairs

Lieutenant General (USA) Thomas N. Burnette, Jr., Deputy Chief of Staff for Operations and Plans, U.S. Army

Lieutenant General (USA) Kevin P. Byrnes, Commander, 1st Cavalry Division

Lieutenant General (USA) Larry R. Ellis, Commander, 1st Armored Division

Major General (USA) Richard A. Cody, Assistant Division Commander, 4th Infantry Division, and Deputy Commander, Task Force Hawk

Major General (USAF) William S. Hinton, Jr., Commander, 3rd Air Force and Joint Task Force Shining Hope

Mr. Kenneth Huffman, Director, Defense Operations Division, U.S. Mission to NATO

Brigadier General (USA) Peter W. Chiarelli, Executive Officer to Supreme Allied Commander Europe

Brigadier General (USA) James D. Thurman, Assistant Chief of Staff for Plans and Policy, Allied Air Forces Southern Europe

Brigadier General (USA) Mitchell H. Stevenson, Deputy Chief of Staff for Logistics, U.S. Army Europe and Seventh Army

Brigadier General (USA) William H. Brandenburg, Chief of Staff, V Corps, U.S. Army Europe and Seventh Army

Other Individuals, United States

Ms. Karen Decker

Ms. Jacqueline Henningsen

Mr. Arley McCormick

Dr. Greg Pedlow

Colonel Raymond T. Odierno

Colonel Douglas MacGregor

Colonel Charles Borchini

Colonel Mark Kimmitt

Colonel Pete Palmer

Colonel Gregory Kaufmann

Captain Robert Blandford

Colonel Patrick Sweeney

Colonel Oliver Hunter

Colonel Daniel Hahn

Colonel Edward Menard

Colonel Alan Stolberg

Colonel Clifton Bray

Lieutenant Colonel Robert Everson

Lieutenant Colonel Dennis O'Brian

Lieutenant Colonel Thomas Riley

Lieutenant Colonel Thomas Johnson

Lieutenant Colonel William Stark

Commander Brian Faulhaber

NATO Allies

Dr. John Catherall (U.K.)

Mr. Geoffrey Hawkins (U.K.)

Mr. Phillip Jones (U.K.)

Mr. Simon Marsh (U.K.)

Dr. James Moffat (U.K.)

Mr. Edward Vandeputte (Belgium)

Colonel Graham Binns (U.K.)

Lieutenant Colonel Hugh Toler (U.K.)

Lieutenant Colonel Kees DeMoel (Netherlands)

Lieutenant Colonel Laslo Makk (Hungary)

BIBLIOGRAPHY

NOTE: *As previously indicated in the report, not all material listed is in the public domain.*

Abramowitz, Sheppie, International Rescue Committee, interview conducted by Cheryl Benard, RAND, on September 17, 1999.

Abuzayd, Karen Konig, Regional Representative, United Nations High Commissioner for Refugees, interview conducted by Cheryl Bernard, RAND, October 13, 1999.

"Agreed Points on Russian Participation in KFOR," June 18, 1999. Available at *http://www.kforonline.com.*

Albright, Madeleine, Secretary of State, "U.S. and NATO Policy Toward the Crisis in Kosovo," Statement before the Senate Foreign Relations Committee, April 20, 1999.

Albright, Madeleine, Secretary of State, and Robin Cook, U.K. Secretary of State for Foreign and Commonwealth Affairs, Op-ed Piece, *Washington Post,* Washington, D.C., May 16, 1999.

Allied Forces Southern Europe, "Fact Sheet, Operation Deny Flight," Headquarters, Allied Forces Southern Europe, Naples, Italy, September 1996.

Allied Forces Southern Europe, Italy, "Operation Determined Guarantor." Available at *http://www.afsouth.nato.int/operations/ detguarantor/Guarantor.htm.*

Allied Forces Southern Europe, Italy, "Operation Eagle Eye." Available at *http://www.afsouth.nato.int/operations/deteagle/Eagle.htm.*

American Embassy Tiranë, electrical message, dated 221352Z April 1999.

Amnesty International, *"Collateral Damage" or Unlawful Killings? Violations of the Laws of War by NATO during Operation Allied Force*, London, England, June 7, 2000.

Antonenko, Oksana, "Russia, NATO, and European Security After Kosovo," *Survival*, Vol. 41, No. 4 (Winter 1999–2000), pp. 124–144.

Arkin, William M., "Civilian Deaths in the NATO Air Campaign," Human Rights Watch, *http://hrw.org/hrw/reports/2000/nato.*

Arkin, William, M., "Smart Bombs, Dumb Targeting?" *Bulletin of the Atomic Scientists*, May/June 2000.

Army Staff briefings, June–July 1999.

Ash, Timothy Garton, "Anarchy & Madness," *New York Review of Books*, February 10, 2000, pp. 48–53.

Ash, Timothy Garton, "Cry, the Dismembered Country," *New York Review of Books*, January 14, 1999, pp. 29–33.

Ash, Timothy Garton, "Kosovo and Beyond," *New York Review of Books*, June 24, 1999, pp. 4–7.

Attack Helicopter Operations, FM (Field Manual) 1-112, Washington, D.C.: Headquarters, Department of the Army, 1997.

Aubin, Stephen, "Operation Allied Force: War or 'Coercive Diplomacy'?" *Strategic Review*, Summer 1999, pp. 4–12.

Bacon, Kenneth H., Assistant Secretary of Defense, "[Department of Defense] News Briefing," Pentagon, Washington, D.C., April 4, 1999.

Bacon, Kenneth H., Assistant Secretary of Defense, interview, Pentagon, Washington, D.C., March 27, 1999.

Balz, Dan, "U.S. Consensus Grows to Send in Ground Troops," *Washington Post*, April 6, 1999.

Barry, John, "Newsweek and the 14 Tanks," *Air Force Magazine*, August 2000, pp. 6–7.

Barry, John, and Evan Thomas, "The Kosovo Cover-Up," *Newsweek*, May 15, 2000, pp. 23–26.

Becker, Elizabeth, "Not Enough Troops in Kosovo, NATO Says," *The New York Times*, February 26, 2000.

Beeston, Richard, Michael Evans, and Ian Brodie, "Pentagon Holds Mitrovica Unit," *London Times*, February 29, 2000.

Bender, Bryan, "US Weapons Shortages Risks Success in Kosovo, *Jane's Defence Weekly*, Washington, D.C., October 6, 1999.

Bender, Bryan, "USA Outlines Post-Kosovo Investments," *Jane's Defence Weekly*, Washington, D.C., Vol. 32, No. 16, October 20, 1999.

Bender, Bryan, and Andrew Koch, "Army Seeks Dual Route to Medium-Sized Force," *Jane's Defence Weekly*, Washington, D.C., Vol. 32, No. 16, October 20, 1999.

Berger, Samuel R., Remarks at the United States Institute of Peace, Washington, D.C., September 30, 1999.

Berger, Samuel R., Assistant to the President for National Security, White House Briefing Room, Washington, D.C., March 25, 1999.

Bowers, Stephen, and Marion Doss, Jr., "Low Intensity Conflict in the Balkans," *Armed Forces Journal International*, May 1999, pp. 28–34.

Boyd, Terry, "Law, Order Imminent, KFOR Commander Vows," *European Stars and Stripes*, January 5, 2000, p. 3.

Brinkley, C. Mark, "The Iron Fist of our Nation's Resolve," *Sea Power*, November 1999, pp. 41–43.

Bugajski, Janusz, "Ripple Effect," *Armed Forces Journal International*, May 1999, pp. 38–40.

Burleigh, A. Peter, Ambassador, United Nations Security Council Statement on Macedonia, U.S. Information Service (USIS) Washington File, February 25, 1999. Available at *http://www.eucom.mil/europe/macedonia/usis/99feb25.htm*.

Burns, Robert, "US to Limit Kosovo Patrols," Associated Press, February 29, 2000.

Butler, Amy, "DOD, State Dept. Debate Whether 'Weaponized' UAV Would Violate Treaty," *Inside the Air Force*, December 8, 2000, p. 1.

Ceku, Agim, Lieutenant General, Chief of Staff, UCK, statement, September 20, 1999. Available at *http://www.kforonline.com*.

Center for Army Lessons Learned, "Task Force Hawk in Operations Allied Force," Initial Impressions Report, Fort Leavenworth, KS, September 1999.

Chairman of the Joint Chiefs of Staff, *Command and Control for Joint Air Operations*, Washington, D.C.: Joint Pub 3-56.1, November 1994.

Chairman of the Joint Chiefs of Staff, *Doctrine for Joint Interdiction Operations*, Washington, D.C.: Joint Pub 3-03, April 1997.

Chairman of the Joint Chiefs of Staff, *Joint Tactics, Techniques, and Procedures for Close Air Support (CAS)*, Washington, D.C.: Joint Pub 3-09.3, December 1995.

Chandler, Robert, "Open Skies Over Kosovo," *Armed Forces Journal International*, May 1999, p. 16.

Cilluffo, Frank, and George Salmoiraghi, "And the Winner Is . . . The Albanian Mafia," *The Washington Quarterly*, Autumn 1999–2000, pp. 21–25.

Clark, Wesley K., "Risking the Alliance," *Washington Post*, December 8, 2000, p. A41.

Clark, Wesley K., General (USA), and Brigadier General (USAF) John D. W. Corley, Press Conference on the Kosovo Strike Assessment, Headquarters, Supreme Allied Command Europe, Mons, Belgium, September 16, 1999. Available at *www.eucom.mn/operations/ai/nato/meabriefing.num*.

Clark, Wesley K., General (USA), interviewed by Brigadier General John Corley (USAF), Colonel Roy Sikes (USAF), and Anthony Tolin, on October 1, 1999.

Clark, Wesley K., General, Supreme Allied Commander Europe, and Lieutenant General Michael Short, testimony before the Senate Subcommittee on Armed Services, "Lessons Learned from Military Operations and Relief Efforts in Kosovo," October 21, 1999.

Clark, Wesley K., *Waging Modern War*, New York: Public Affairs, 2001.

Clark, Wesley, General (USA), "When Force Is Necessary: NATO's Military Response to the Kosovo Crisis," *NATO Review* (Web edition), Vol. 47, No. 4 (Winter 1999), pp. 14–18.

Clinton, William J., President of the United States, letter to the Speaker of the House of Representatives and the President of the Senate, White House, Washington, D.C., April 3, 1999, released April 5, 1999.

Clinton, William J., President, "A Just and Necessary War," *The New York Times*, May 23, 1999.

Clinton, William J., President, "Address to the Nation," March 24, 1999.

Clinton, William J., President, and Secretary of State William S. Cohen, Roosevelt Room, Washington, D.C., April 5, 1999.

Clinton, William J., President, interview with Dan Rather, Columbia Broadcasting System, The White House, Washington, D.C., March 31, 1999.

Clinton, William J., President, report to Congress under section 8115, March 25, 1999; second report submitted on April 4, 1999, "Text of a Letter from the President," The White House, Office of the Press Secretary, March 25 and April 4, 1999.

Clinton, William J., President, Statement on the Department of Defense Appropriations Act, White House Press Office, October 17, 1998.

Cody, Richard, Brigadier General, Assistant Division Commander, 4th Infantry Division at Fort Hood, "Task Force Hawk—Lessons Learned in Albania," at request of General Eric Shinseki, Vice Chief of Staff, Army, June 16, 1999.

Cohen, William S., and General (USA) Henry H. Shelton, Joint Statement on the Kosovo After Action Report, Senate Armed Services Committee, Washington, D.C., October 14, 1999.

Cohen, William S., General (USA) Henry H. Shelton, and Major General (USAF) Charles F. "Chuck" Wald, "Operation Allied Force," Department of Defense News Briefing, Pentagon, Washington, D.C., 4:05 P.M., June 10, 1999.

Cohen, William S., interview, *Frontline,* PBS,

Cohen, William S., Secretary of Defense, and Chairman of the Joint Chiefs of Staff General Henry Shelton, Department of Defense News Briefing, Pentagon, Washington, D.C., March 24, 1999.

Commander, Kosovo Forces, Kosovo Protection Corps, "Statement of Principles." Available at *http://www.kforonline.com.*

Cook, Nick, "Serb Air War Changes Gear," *Jane's Defence Weekly*, Vol. 31, No. 14 (April 7, 1999), pp. 24–25.

Correll, John, "Assumptions Fall in Kosovo," *AIR FORCE Magazine*, June 1999, p. 4.

Correll, John, "Lessons Drawn and Quartered," *AIR FORCE Magazine*, December 1999, p. 2.

Daalder, Ivo H., and Michael E. O'Hanlon, "Unlearning the Lessons of Kosovo," *Foreign Policy*, Fall 1999, pp. 128–140.

Daalder, Ivo H., and Michael E. O'Hanlon, *Winning Ugly, NATO's War to Save Kosovo*, Washington, D.C.: Brookings Institution Press, 2000.

Danner, Mark, "Kosovo: The Meaning of Victory," *New York Review of Books*, July 15, 1999, pp. 53–54.

Department of Defense Appropriations Act, Conference Report, 105th Congress, Washington, D.C., Summer 1999.

"The Deployment in Kosovo," *Army*, September 1999, p. 66.

DoD Dictionary of Military and Associated Terms, Washington, D.C.: Joint Publication 1-02, Joint Chiefs of Staff, 2000.

Drozdiak, William, "NATO Leaders Struggle to Find a Winning Strategy," *Washington Post*, April 1, 1999.

Drozdiak, William, "Yugoslav Troops Devastated by Attack," *Washington Post*, June 9, 1999.

Ellis, James O., Admiral (USN), "A View from the Top," Briefing, Headquarters, U.S. Naval Forces, Europe, in Naples, Italy, undated, unclassified.

Erlanger, Steven, "NATO Was Closer to Ground War in Kosovo Than Widely Realized," *The New York Times*, November 7, 1999.

Evans, Michael, "Dark Victory," *U.S. Naval Institute Proceedings*, September 1999, pp. 33–37.

Federal Republic of Yugoslavia, Agreement on Sub-Regional Arms Control, Information on the Army of Yugoslavia, Annual Data Exchange, Valid as of January 1, 1999.

Federal Republic of Yugoslavia, Information on Armaments Limited by the Agreement on Sub-Regional Arms Control in Federal Republic of Yugoslavia, Entry into Force, January 1, 2000.

Finnegan, William, "The Next War," *The New Yorker*, September 20, 1999, pp. 60–72.

Fiorenza, Nicholas, "Identity Crisis," *Armed Forces Journal International*, September 1999, pp. 66–70.

Follath, Erich, "Die Belgrad Party," *Der Spiegel*, Vol. 46 (November 15, 1999), pp. 218–222.

Fox, Michael R., "United Nations High Commissioner for Refugees Daily HUMRO [Humanitarian Relief Operations] Airlift Situation Report," United Nations Air Coordination Cell, Geneva, Switzerland, May 15, 1999.

Friedman, Norman, "Did Kosovo Teach Us Anything," *U.S. Naval Institute Proceedings*, August 1999, pp. 91–92.

Friedman, Norman, "Was Kosovo the Future," *U.S. Naval Institute Proceedings*, January 2000, pp. 6–8.

Fulghum, David A., "Electronic Bombs Darken Belgrade," *Aviation Week & Space Technology*, May 10, 1999.

Fulghum, David A., "Glide Bombs Modified to Hit Through Clouds," *Aviation Week & Space Technology*, June 7, 1999.

Fulghum, David A., "Improved Missiles Trigger Jammer Need," *Aviation Week & Space Technology*, September 27, 1999.

Fulghum, David A., "NATO Unprepared for Electronic Combat," *Aviation Week & Space Technology*, May 10, 1999.

Fulghum, David A., "Pentagon Gets Lock on F-177 Shootdown," *Aviation Week & Space Technology*, April 19, 1999, pp. 28–30.

Fulghum, David A., and Robert Wall, "UAV Weapons Focus of Debate," *Aviation Week & Space Technology*, September 25, 2000, pp. 29–30.

Gandy, Bruce, Lieutenant Colonel, et al., "The Kosovo Commitment," *Marine Corps Gazette*, November 1999, pp. 44–65 (eleven short articles).

Ganyard, Stephen, Lieutenant Colonel, "The Price of Commitment," *Marine Corps Gazette*, January 2000, pp. 63–64.

Garamone, Jim, "NATO Expands Target List, Reserve Call-Up Near," American Forces Press Service, April 23, 1999.

General Framework Agreement for Peace in Bosnia and Hertzegovina (also known as the Dayton Agreement, signed in Paris, December 14, 1995. Available at *http://www.ohr.int/gfa/gfa-home.htm*.

"General Jackson Rejects Criticism of British Forces," *RFE/RL Newsline* (Radio Free Europe/Radio Liberty), January 4, 2000. Available at *http://www.rferl.org.newsline*.

Graham, Bradley, "The Explanation in Washington; U.S. Analysts Misread, Relied on Outdated Maps," *Washington Post*, May 11, 1999, p. A17.

Grant, Rebecca, "Airpower Made It Work," *AIR FORCE Magazine*, November 1999, pp. 30–37.

Grant, Rebecca, "The Kosovo Campaign: Aerospace Power Made It Work," *The Air Force Association*, September 1999.

Guicherd, Catherine, "International Law and the War in Kosovo," *Survival*, Vol. 41, No. 2 (Summer 1999), pp. 19–34.

Hagen, William, "The Balkan's Lethal Nationalisms," *Foreign Affairs*, July/August 1999, pp. 52–64.

Hamilton, Douglas, "Politics May Sway Military Choice on Kosovo," Reuters, December 1, 1999.

Hamre, John, Deputy Secretary of Defense, and General (USAF) Joe Ralston, Vice Chairman of the Joint Chiefs of Staff, "Operation Allied Force—After Action Review: Lessons Learned from Kosovo," Winter 1999/2000. Available at *http://www.defenselink. mil/specials/lessons*.

Heads of State and Government participating in the meeting of the North Atlantic Council in Washington, D.C., April 23 and 24, 1999, "Statement on Kosovo," NATO Press Release S-1(99)62, Washington, D.C., April 23, 1999.

Hedges, Chris, "Kosovo's Next Masters," *Foreign Affairs*, May/June 1999, pp. 24–42.

Hoffman, Stanley, "On Kosovo: What Is to Be Done?" *New York Review of Books*, May 20, 1999, pp. 17–18.

Holbrooke, Richard, *To End a War*, New York: Random House, 1998.

Hooper, James, "Kosovo: America's Balkan Problem," *Current History*, April 1999, pp. 159–164.

Hosmer, Stephen T., *The Conflict Over Kosovo: Why Milosevic Decided to Settle When He Did*, Santa Monica, CA: RAND, MR-1351-AF, 2001.

Ignatieff, Michael, "The Virtual Commander: How NATO Invented a New Kind of War," *The New Yorker*, August 2, 1999, pp. 30–36.

IISS, "Air-Power over Kosovo," *Strategic Comments*, Vol. 5, No. 7 (September 1999).

IISS, "NATO's Campaign in Yugoslavia," *Strategic Comments*, Vol. 5, No. 3 (April 1999).

Institute for National Security Studies, *Peace Operations Forum*, Washington, D.C.: National Defense University, April 12, 2000.

International Crisis Group (ICG), "Starting from Scratch in Kosovo: The Honeymoon Is Over," *ICG Balkans Report No. 83*, December 10, 1999.

Mission Analysis Tracking & Tabulation System, Operation Allied Force Data, Studies & Analysis, U.S. Air Forces in Europe, Ramstein, Germany.

Jackson, Michael, General, speech during NATO/KFOR Transfer of Authority Ceremony, Pristina, October 12, 1999.

Jane's Armour and Artillery, 1998–99, London, New York: Jane's, serial.

Joint Chiefs of Staff, "Operation Allied Force," Briefing, Washington, D.C., June 10, 1999. Available at *www.defenselink.mil/news/ Jun1999.*

Joint Tactics, Techniques, and Procedures for Close Air Support (CAS), Washington, D.C.: Joint Pub 3-09.3, Joint Chiefs of Staff, 1995, p. I-1.

Judah, Tim, "Impasse in Kosovo," *New York Review of Books*, October 8, 1998, pp. 4–6.

Judah, Tim, "Kosovo: Peace Now," *New York Review of Books*, August 12, 1999, pp. 22–28.

Judah, Tim, "Kosovo's Road to War," *Survival*, Vol. 41, No. 2 (Summer 1999), pp. 5–18.

Judah, Tim, *Kosovo, War and Revenge,* New Haven, CT: Yale University Press, 2000.

Jundt, Tony, "Inside the Kosovo Liberation Army," *New York Review of Books,* June 10, 1999, pp. 19–23.

Jundt, Tony, "On Kosovo: The Reason Why," *New York Review of Books,* April 22, 1999, p. 16.

Kandebo, Stanley W., "Boeing Premieres UCAV Demonstrator, *Aviation Week & Space Technology,* October 2, 2000, pp. 30–33.

Kandebo, Stanley W., "SEAD [suppression of enemy air defense], Other Ground Attack Capabilities Planned for UCAVs," *Aviation Week & Space Technology,* October 2, 2000, pp. 30–31.

KFOR Online, *http://www.kforonline.com.*

Kitfield, James, "Another Look at the War that Was," *AIR FORCE Magazine,* October 1999, pp. 39–43.

"Kosovo Commitment," series of articles, *Marine Corps Gazette,* November 1999.

"Kosovo—The Task Force Commander's Viewpoint," *Army,* September 1999, p. 58.

Kozaryn, Linda D., "Serb Forces Abduct Three U.S. Soldiers," American Forces Information Service, April 1, 1999. Available at *http://www.eucom.mil.operations/tfs/index.htm.*

Krauthammer, Charles, "The Short, Unhappy Life of Humanitarian War," *The National Interest,* No. 57 (Fall 1999), pp. 5–8.

Lambeth, Benjamin S., *NATO's Air War for Kosovo: A Strategic and Operational Assessment,* Santa Monica, CA: RAND, MR-1365-AF, 2001.

Lidy, A. Martin, et al., *Bosnia Air Drop Study,* Alexandria, VA: Institute for Defense Analyses, IDA Paper P-3474, 1999.

Lowrey, Nathan S., "Peacekeeping Operations in Kosovo: The 26th Marine Expeditionary Unit During Operation Joint Guardian," *Marine Corps Gazette,* December 1999, pp. 57–63.

Luttwak, Edward, "Give War a Chance," *Foreign Affairs*, July/August 1999, pp. 36–44.

Lynch, J.D., Jr., *"Truth in Kosovo," U.S. Naval Institute Proceedings*, August 1999, p. 2.

Macdonald, Scott, "The Mission Must Be Worth the Risk," *U.S. Naval Institute Proceedings*, September 1999, pp. 27–29.

Mandelbaum, Michael, "A Perfect Failure," *Foreign Affairs*, September/October 1999, pp. 2–8.

Marcus, Jonathan, "A Distant Trumpet," *The Washington Quarterly*, Summer 1999, pp. 7–10.

McManus, Doyle, "Clinton's Massive Ground Invasion That Almost Was," *Los Angeles Times*, June 9, 2000.

McPeak, Merrill, General, "The Kosovo Result," *Armed Forces Journal International*, September 1999, pp. 62–64.

Meilinger, Phillip, Colonel, "Gradual Escalation," *Armed Forces Journal International*, October 1999, p. 18.

Mertens, Richard, "Keeping Order on Kosovo Border," *Christian Science Monitor*, March 17, 2000.

"Military-Technical Agreement Between the International Security Force ("KFOR") and the Government of the Federal Republic of Yugoslavia and the Federal Republic of Serbia," June 9, 1999. Available at *http://www.kforonline.com*.

Morin, Richard, "Poll Shows Most Americans Want Negotiations on Kosovo, *Washington Post*, May 18, 1999.

Morris, Nicholas, "Origins of a Crisis," *Refugees,* Vol. 3, No. 116, United Nations High Commissioner for Refugees, Geneva, Switzerland, 1999.

Mortens, Richard, "Keeping Order on Kosovo Border," *Christian Science Monitor*, March 17, 2000, p. 6.

Murphy, Daniel J., Admiral (USN), "The Navy in the Balkans," *AIR FORCE Magazine*, December 1999, pp. 48–49 (excerpted from testimony, Senate Armed Services Committee, October 13, 1999).

Myers, Gene, and Lieutenant General Thad Wolfe, "The Price of Greatness: Air Power in the Balkans," *Strategic Review*, Summer 1999, pp. 13–16.

National Interest, No. 57 (Fall 1999), pp. 9–15.

"NATO: Assessing the Damage," *Newsweek International*, December 20, 1999.

Naumann, Klaus, Press Conference, NATO Headquarters, May 4, 1999. Available at *http://www.nato.int/docu/speech/1999/ s990504c.htm.*

Neier, Aryeh, "Impasse in Kosovo," *New York Review of Books*, September 25, 1997, pp. 51–53.

Nordwall, Bruce C., and Robert Wall, "Navy Pursues Upgrades to Antiradar Weapon," *Aviation Week & Space Technology*, October 2, 2000, pp. 64–66.

North Atlantic Council, "Statement on Kosovo," Press Release S-1(99)62, Heads of State and Government participants, Washington, D.C., April 23, 1999.

North Atlantic Council, NATO Press Statement (1999) 040, March 23, 1999, and "Statement by Secretary General Dr. Javier Solana," March 24, 1999.

O'Connor, Mike, "NATO War Planes Give Warning to Milosevic," *The New York Times*, June 16, 1998, p. 1.

Organization for Security and Cooperation in Europe, "Kosovo As Seen, As Told, The Human Rights Findings of the OSCE Kosovo Verification Mission," 1999. Available at *http//www.osce.org/ kosovo/reports/hr.*

Perlez, Jane, "Clinton and the Joint Chiefs of Staff to Discuss Ground Invasion," *The New York Times*, June 2, 1999.

Perlez, Jane, "NATO Raid Hits China Embassy; Beijing Cites 'Barbarian Act'; Allies Admit Striking Hospital," *The New York Times*, May 8, 1999, pp. A1, A6.

Pirnie, Bruce, *Civilians and Soldiers, Achieving Better Coordination*, Santa Monica, CA: RAND, MR-1026-SRF, 1999.

Pond, Elizabeth, "Kosovo: Catalyst for Europe," *The Washington Quarterly*, Autumn 1999, pp. 77–92.

Priest, Dana, "A Decisive Battle That Never Was," *Washington Post*, September 19, 1999, p. A1.

Priest, Dana, "Army's Apache Helicopter Rendered Impotent in Kosovo," *Washington Post*, December 29, 1999, p. A1.

Priest, Dana, "France Acted as Group Skeptic," *Washington Post*, September 20, 1999.

Priest, Dana, "NATO Concedes Its Bombs Likely Killed Refugees," *Washington Post*, April 20, 1999, p. A19.

Prina, L. Edward, "Air War Kosovo," *Sea Power*, November 1999, pp. 47–50.

Public Law 105-262, Department of Defense Appropriations Act, 1999, 105th Congress; Department of Defense Appropriations Act, 1999—Conference Report.

Rater, Philippe, "NATO Leaders Resigned to Giving Russia Share in Kosovo," Agence France Presse, June 14, 1999.

Record, Jeffrey, "Operation Allied Force: Yet Another Wake-Up Call for the Army?" *Parameters*, Winter 1999–2000, pp. 15–23.

"Report of the Secretary-General on the United Nations Preventive Force Pursuant to Security Council Resolution 1186 (1998)," S/1999/161, February 12, 1999. Available at *http://www.un.org/ Docs/sc/reports/1999/s1999161.htm*.

Richter, Paul, "Bunker-Busters Aim at Heart of Leadership," *Los Angeles Times*, May 5, 1999.

Richter, Paul, "Use of Ground Troops Not Fully Ruled Out," *Los Angeles Times*, March 29, 1999.

Ripley, Tim, "Kosovo: A Bomb Damage Assessment," *Jane's Intelligence Review*, September 1999, pp. 10–13.

Robbins, Carla Anne, and Thomas E. Ricks, "Time Is Running Out If Invasion Is to Remain Option Before Winter," *Wall Street Journal*, May 21, 1999.

Roberts Amendment, Number 3393, Department of Defense Appropriations Act of 1999, July 30, 1998.

Roberts Amendment, Section 8115 of Public Law 105-262, Department of Defense Appropriations Act of 1999.

Roberts, Adam, "NATO's 'Humanitarian War' in Kosovo," *Survival*, Vol. 41, No. 3 (Autumn 1999), pp. 102–123.

Robertson, (Lord), "Kosovo: An Account of the Crisis," London, U.K. Ministry of Defence Paper, October 6, 1999, p. 2.

Robertson, Charles T., Jr., General (USAF), Commander in Chief, U.S. Transportation Command, "Statement to the House Armed Services Committee," October 26, 1999.

Roche, Andrew, "Law and Order Is Kosovo's Achilles Heel," Reuters, December 27, 1999.

Rodman, Peter, "The Fallout from Kosovo," *Foreign Affairs*, July/August 1999, pp. 45–51.

"Russian and NATO Forces in Stand-off Over Kosovo," *Financial Times*, June 12, 1999, p. 1.

Ryan, Michael E., General (USAF), *The Air War over Serbia*, Ramstein Air Force Base, Germany: Studies and Analysis Directorate, United States Air Force in Europe, 2000. Available at *http://www.af.mil*.

Scales, Robert, Major General, "From Korea to Kosovo," *Armed Forces Journal International*, December 1999, pp. 36–41.

Scott, William B., "Apache, Comanche Share Technology," *Aviation Week & Space Technology*, November 6, 2000, pp. 65–66.

Scott, William B., "Pentagon Mum About F-117 Loss," *Aviation Week & Space Technology*, April 5, 1999, p. 31.

Seigle, Greg, "Allied Force Applied to Serbia," *Jane's Defence Weekly*, Vol. 31, No. 13 (March 31, 1999), p. 3.

Sharer, Wayne, Commander, "Command and Control: The Navy War Over Kosovo," *U.S. Naval Institute Proceedings*, October 1999.

Shea, Jamie, and Brigadier General Giuseppe Marani, Briefing, NATO Headquarters, Brussels, Belgium, April 16, 1999.

Shinseki, Eric K., General, "The Army Vision: Soldiers on Point for the Nation . . . Persuasive in Peace, Invincible in War," Office of Chief of Staff vision statement. Available at *http://www.hqda.army.mil/ ocsa/vision.htm.*

Short, Michael, Lieutenant General (USAF), testimony before the Senate Committee on Armed Services, Washington, D.C., October 21, 1999.

Silber, Laura, and Allan Little, *Yugoslavia, Death of a Nation*, New York: Penguin Books, 1995.

Sligh, Robert, "Joint Task Force—Shining Hope Chronology," Command Historian, April 1999. Available in electronic form at Headquarters, 3rd Air Force, Mildenhall, U.K.

Smith, Brantley, "On Kosovo," *U.S. Naval Institute Proceedings*, January 2000, pp. 2–4.

Smith, Daniel, Colonel (USA, ret.), "When Numbers Fall Short," *CDI Weekly Defense Monitor*, November 12, 1999.

Smith, R. Jeffrey, "Accord on Kosovo Remains Elusive," *Washington Post*, October 12, 1998, pp. A14, A22.

Smith, R. Jeffrey, "Home Sweet Home in Kosovo: High-Security U.S. Base Will Have All the Creature Comforts," *Washington Post*, October 5, 1999, p. 11.

Smith, R. Jeffrey, "Serbs Tried to Cover Up Massacre," *Washington Post*, January 28, 1999, pp. A1, A24.

Solana, Javier, "NATO's Success in Kosovo," *Foreign Affairs*, November/December 1999, pp. 114–120.

Solana, Javier, NATO Secretary General, Press Statement, Brussels, Belgium, March 24, 1999.

Spinney, Frank, "Learning the Lessons We Want to Learn?" *U.S. Naval Institute Proceedings*, September 1999, p. 6.

Spolar, Christine, "NATO Planes Deliver Hope to Albanians," *Washington Post*, June 16, 1998, pp. A1, A25.

Steele, Dennis, "Kosovo: A Special Report," *Army*, September 1999, pp. 16ff.

Steinberg, James, "A Perfect Polemic: Blind to Reality on Kosovo," *Foreign Affairs*, November/December 1999, pp. 128–133.

Studies and Analysis Division, U.S. Air Force Europe, *Air War Over Serbia*, April 2000.

Tilford, Earl, "Operation Allied Force and the Role of Air Power," *Parameters*, Winter 1999–2000, pp. 24–38.

Tirpak, John A., "Airlift Reality Check," *AIR FORCE Magazine*, December 1999, pp. 31–36.

Tirpak, John A., "Deliberate Force," *AIR FORCE Magazine*, October 1997, pp. 36–43.

Tirpak, John A., "Short's View of the Air Campaign," *AIR FORCE Magazine*, September 1999, pp. 43–47.

Tirpak, John A., "The First Six Weeks," *AIR FORCE Magazine*, June 1999, pp. 27–29.

Tirpak, John A., "With Stealth in the Balkans," *AIR FORCE Magazine*, October 1999, pp. 23–28.

Tirpak, John, "The NATO Way of War," *AIR FORCE Magazine*, December 1999, pp. 24–27.

Tirpak, John, "Victory in Kosovo," *AIR FORCE Magazine,* July 1999, pp. 24–27.

Tirpak, John, "With Stealth in the Balkans," *AIR FORCE Magazine,* October 1999, pp. 23–28.

Tissue, Phillip, Lieutenant Colonel, "21 Minutes to Belgrade," *U.S. Naval Institute Proceedings,* September 1999, p. 38–40.

Troebst, Stefan, "The Kosovo Conflict," Appendix 1C in SIPRI Yearbook 1999, *Armaments, Disarmament, and International Security,* Stockholm International Peace Research Institute, Oxford, New York: Oxford University Press, 1999, pp. 47–62.

U.K. House of Commons, Session 1999–2000, Foreign Affairs Committee, *Fourth Report, Kosovo,* London, printed May 23, 2000. Available at *http://www.publications.parliament.uk/pa/cm199900/cmselect/cmfaff.*

U.S. Agency for International Development (USAID), Kosovo Crisis Fact Sheet #64, Washington, D.C., June 3, 1999. Available at *http://www.info.usaid.gov/num_response/ofda/kosofs64.*

U.S. Army Europe and Seventh Army, "Operation Allied Force Joint After Action Report Executive Summary," undated.

U.S. Army Europe Lessons Learned Office, Draft, "Operation Victory Hawk After Action Report," November 3, 1999.

U.S. Department of Defense News Briefing, Department of Defense Link, April 4, 1999.

U.S. Department of Defense News Briefing, Statement by Assistant Secretary of Defense for Public Affairs Kenneth Bacon, Washington, D.C., March 23, 1999.

U.S. Department of Defense, "U.S. Attack Helicopters and Multiple Launch Rocket Systems to Deploy in Support of Operation Allied Force," Department of Defense Press Release No. 145-99, April 4, 1999.

U.S. Department of Defense, Report to Congress, *Kosovo/Operation Allied Force After Action Report,* Washington, D.C., January 31, 2000.

U.S. Department of State Press Statement, "Secretary Albright Meets With Foreign Ministers Regarding the Situation in Kosovo and Surrounding Region," April 3, 1999.

U.S. European Command Logistics and Security Assistance Directorate briefing, "Kosovo Campaign Logistics," ECJ4, July 1999, September 15, 1999.

U.S. General Accounting Office, *Balkans Security, Current and Projected Factors Affecting Regional Security*, Briefing Report to the Chairman, Committee on Armed Services, House of Representatives, GAO/NSIAD-00-125BR, Washington, D.C., April 2000.

U.S. Mission to NATO, *Kosovo Crisis, Summary Of Key Events And North.*

Undertaking of Demilitarisation and Transformation by the UCK, June 20, 1999. Available at *http://www.kforonline.com.*

UNEP and Habitat Joint press release, "Balkans Task Force Recommends Immediate Environmental Action as Part of Humanitarian Aid: Four Environmental Hotspots found in Serbia," For Information Only—Not an Official Fecord, October 14, 1999. Available at *http://www.grid.unep.ch:80/btf/pressrelease/unep1410.html.*

United Nations Security Council, Letter dated June 4, 1999, from the Permanent Representative of France to the United Nations, addressed to the Secretary-General, enclosing the Rambouillet Accords*: Interim Agreement for Peace and Self-Government in Kosovo*, S/1999/648, June 7, 1999.

United Nations, peacekeeping information. Available at *http://www.un.org/peace/kosovo/pages/kosovo_status.htm.*

United Nations, UN Security Council Resolution 1244, S/RES/1244(1999), June 10, 1999. Available at *http://www.un.org/docs/scres/1999/99sc1244.htm.*

United Nations, United Nations Security Council Resolution 795, December 11, 1992. Available at *http://www.un.org/Depts/DPKO/Missions/unpred_p.htm.*

UNMIK (United Nations Interim Administration in Kosovo), "Bring Peace to Kosovo: Mandate and Tasks," undated. Available at *http://www.un.org/peace/kosovo/pages/kosovo12.htm.*

UNMIK, "Bring Peace to Kosovo: Status Report," January 13, 2000. Available at *http://www.un.org/peace/kosovo/pages/kosovo_status.htm.*

UNMIK/RE/1999/8, "On the Establishment of the Kosovo Protection Corps." Available at *http://www.kforonline.com.*

UNMIK/REG/1999/1, "On the Authority of the Interim Administration in Kosovo," July 25, 1999. Available at *http://www.un.org/peace/kosovo/pages/regulations/reg1.htm.*

Wall, Robert, "Air War Drives EA-6B Upgrades," *Aviation Week & Space Technology,* May 31, 1999, p. 68.

Wall, Robert, "Army Intelligence Aircraft to Support Ground Forces," *Aviation Week & Space Technology,* May 10, 1999, p. 39.

Wall, Robert, "E-2Cs Become Battle Managers with Reduced AEW [Aerospace Expeditionary Wing] Role," *Aviation Week & Space Technology,* May 10, 1999, p. 38.

Wall, Robert, "F/A-18 Recce System Heads for Kosovo," *Aviation Week & Space Technology,* May 24, 1999, p. 39.

Wiedemann, Erich, "Frieren und demonstrieren," *Der Spiegel,* Vol. 42, October 18, 1999, pp. 226–229.

Wiedemann, Erich, "Orchester aus Solisten," *Der Spiegel,* Vol. 44, November 1, 1999, pp. 180–181.

Williams, Daniel, "Refugees Killed in Kosovo Attack; NATO Admits Strike; Yugoslavia Says at least 79 Civilians Slain," *Washington Post,* May 15, 1999. p. A1.

Wilson, George C., "Army Admits Its Apache Outfit Was Not Ready Enough to Fight in Kosovo," LEGI-SLATE News Service, Washington, D.C., June 18, 1999.

Winand, Timothy, Major, "On Using Marines in an Interim Police Force Role," *Marine Corps Gazette,* January 2000, pp. 60–62.

Winograd, Erin Q., "4th ID Deputy CG Says Task Force Hawk Has Exposed Aviation Weakness—Cody: First Three Weeks in Albania 'Painful and High-Risk,'" *Inside the Army,* June 21, 1999, p. 1.

Wintour, Patrick, and Peter Beaumont, "Leaks in NATO and Plan Bravo Minus," *London Sunday Observer,* July 18, 1999.

Wintour, Patrick, and Peter Beaumont, "Revealed: The Secret Plan to Invade Kosovo—NATO Ready to Go in as Milosevic Withdrew," *London Sunday Observer,* July 18, 1999.

Zimmerman, Warren, "Milosevic's Final Solution," *New York Review of Books,* June 10, 1999, pp. 41–43.